THIRD WORLD MILITARY EXPENDITURE

TO: KATE, CLARE AND LUCY

THIRD WORLD MILITARY EXPENDITURE

Determinants and Implications

R.D. MCKINLAY

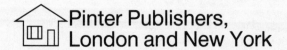Pinter Publishers,
London and New York

First published in Great Britain in 1989 by
Pinter Publishers Limited
25 Floral Street, London WC2E 9DS

British Library Cataloguing in Publication Data

A CIP catalogue record for this book is available from
the British Library.

ISBN 0-86187-721-7

Library of Congress Cataloguing-in-Publication Data

McKinlay, Robert D.
  Third World military expenditure.

  Includes index.
  1. Developing countries—Armed Forces—
Appropriations and expenditures. I. Title.
UA17.M35   1989   355.6'22'091724   88-32104

Typeset by The Castlefield Press Ltd, Wellingborough.
Printed and bound in Great Britain by Biddles Ltd.

Contents

Acknowledgements

This project was funded mainly by a grant from the Economic and Social Research Council. A smaller grant was also received from the Nuffield Foundation. A substantial debt is due for some of the data to the Stockholm International Peace Research Institute and particularly to continuing and kind assistance from Thomas Ohlson. A number of colleagues both at Northwestern University and the University of Lancaster have helped generously in a variety of ways. Particular mention should be made of Al Cohan, Joe Whittaker and Brian Francis. Special thanks are also due to Angela Ingle, who was responsible for most of the typing. Easily the greatest debt, and a very substantial one at that, is due to Peter Dickinson. Peter Dickinson worked on this project as the principal research assistant in an unstinting, industrious, reliable and creative manner. On innumerable occasions, when substantial protests against either the nature of the work itself or my changes of mind and mood would have been entirely in order, not a murmur of protest was made. Peter Dickinson was not only the perfect research assistant but a good companion.

R.D. McKinlay

1 Military Expenditure – A Descriptive Profile

The central preoccupation of this book is an analysis of the behaviour of Third World military expenditure over the post-war period. A discussion and specification of the more detailed objectives and procedures of the study as a whole are reserved for the following chapter. Our objective in this chapter, though important, is quite limited. We aim to provide a descriptive profile of the behaviour of Third World military expenditure, and in so doing to give some appreciation of the major parameters of the central variable or concern of this study.

Though descriptive profiles are in principle eminently straightforward, the details of such profiles can soon become rather overwhelming. In order to avoid any such descriptive overloading, we present our profile under a series of ordering headings.[1]

Point 1

Although the global structure of world military expenditure has not changed enormously over the post-World War II period, Third World countries have come to contribute an increasing share of total world military expenditure which is now far from insignificant

Military systems have experienced massive change over the post-World War II period. Contemporary military arsenals, whether in their conventional or nuclear forms, bear little resemblance to their predecessors of 1950. Global military expenditure, measured in constant values, has also changed markedly, roughly quadrupling from 1950 to 1985.[2]

The structure of world military expenditure, as profiled by states' relative share, has not changed in anything like such a dramatic manner. Indeed, as compared with changes in the international economic system, as profiled by relative shares in trade or investment, for example, the structure of global military expenditure has been relatively stable.

The most striking hallmark of this stability has been the continued dominance of the superpowers. Though the percentage share of each in total world military expenditure has moved slightly downward, the effective oligopolistic positions of the USA and USSR remain essentially intact. Thus, as we can see from Table 1.1, these two states in 1985 still command just over 50 per cent of world military

Table 1.1: Military expenditure of the USA, USSR, other NATO countries and the Third World as a percentage of total world military expenditure, selected years 1950–85

	1950	1955	1960	1965	1970	1975	1980	1985
USA	29.5	43.4	42.3	36.1	34.4	26.3	25.4	30.9
USSR	28.2	22.6	20.3	22.2	24.3	23.8	23.2	22.0
Other NATO	20.9	19.6	21.3	20.4	16.6	17.8	19.8	18.5
Third World	4.7	3.6	5.1	6.3	8.0	14.7	16.6	16.8

spending.[3] If we include the formal allies of these two states, then the oligopolistic position is further enhanced. The combined military expenditure of all NATO and Warsaw Pact countries, as of 1985, constitutes almost three-quarters of total world military expenditure.[4]

While the oligopolistic position of the superpowers has remained essentially undisturbed, Third World countries' share of total world military expenditure has nonetheless increased. As we see from Table 1.1, Third World military expenditure has grown from around one-twentieth to one-sixth. The significance of this one-sixth share depends very much on the point of comparison.

Taking the USA as the point of reference, it could be argued that Third World military expenditure is still somewhat insignificant. With a combined population in excess of ten times that of the USA, Third World countries spend in aggregate only just over half that of the USA. If we moved outside the expenditure realm to consider the weapons systems themselves, then the USA, other things being equal, could effectively destroy all Third World countries while itself receiving very little by way of counter-damage.

On the other hand, if we make a more global comparison, then the change in the position of the Third World becomes rather more significant. As late as 1960 we could still see essentially a three-tiered structure, in which the superpowers were separated by a largely unbridgeable gap from the other NATO countries, which in turn were separated by a similarly unbridgeable gap from Third World countries. Moving into the 1970s and 1980s, it seems more appropriate to think in terms of a two-tiered structure. The top echelon of the superpowers is still separated by a largely unbridgeable gap from other states. The previous two tiers do seem, however, to have fused, albeit in a rather extensive hierarchy. Thus, Third World countries as a whole have a level of military expenditure close to parity with the other NATO countries. Furthermore, although Britain, France and the Federal Republic of Germany spend more on the military than any Third World state, Saudi Arabia, the largest Third World spender, surpasses Italy, the fourth-ranking other NATO power. Furthermore, a sizeable number of Third World states either exceed or closely approximate the levels of expenditure of the Netherlands and Belgium, the countries which in rank order follow Italy.[5]

The fusion argument also holds if we consider not simply levels of expenditure but type of weapons systems. The special pre-eminence of Britain and France in the nuclear area is not shared even by countries such as Germany or Italy, while it is certainly possible, if not probable, that a greater number of Third World states possess at least some nuclear capability. Furthermore, due primarily to pronounced changes in the conventional arms trade and, to a lesser extent, developments in indigenous weapons production, many Third World countries now possess military hardware of equal sophistication to that of the other NATO countries.[6]

The single most important parameter of the global military structure, namely the oligopolistic pre-eminence of the superpowers, has remained largely constant in the post-World War II period. Admittedly at a level of lesser importance, there has, nonetheless, been a marked change in the military status of Third World countries, which has made it rather more appropriate to think in terms of a two- rather than a three-tiered hierarchy. This fusion, as we have termed it, is a not insignificant development.

Point 2

The expansion of mean gross military expenditure follows a 'compound interest' type of growth. Mean relative expenditure is also increasing significantly, indicating an enhanced propensity on the part of Third World countries to commit an increasing proportion of their resources to the military. This relative commitment has since 1970 surpassed that of the NATO countries

In the point above we have tried to gain a perspective on the growth of Third World military expenditure by focusing on an aggregated total, which by virtue of being expressed as a percentage of a world total was given meaning in terms of a growing share on the part of Third World countries. Change in the aggregated total is not, however, a useful basis from which to begin to characterize the precise form of the expansion since the aggregated total reflects to some degree a simple increase in the total number of Third World countries as they become independent. This difficulty can be partly surmounted by focusing on the mean level of military expenditure over time.[7]

Over our period of analysis Third World mean military expenditure increases quite markedly. This increase fits well a semi-logged regression, meaning that military expenditure grows at an expanding annual volume conforming to a constant proportionate increase. This constant proportionate increase is what we mean by a 'compound interest' type of growth.[8]

Other things being equal, to find an expenditure increasing in this way is neither terribly surprising nor particularly instructive. Such a rate of growth, however, can become instructive when it is compared with other expenditures, of which the immediately most useful is GDP. Mean Third World GDP also grows at a proportionate rate, though critically this rate is lower than that of military expenditure (3.9 per cent per annum compared with 5.4 per cent).[9]

Table 1.2: Mean military expenditure in gross (constant 1975 $b)
and relative forms for Third World countries,
selected years 1950–82

	1950	1955	1960	1965	1970	1975	1980	1982
Mean military expenditure	146	172	177	181	269	507	664	846
Mean military expenditure as % mean GDP	3.14	3.25	2.82	3.01	3.66	4.52	3.89	4.66
Mean military expenditure as % GDP	1.90	2.60	3.36	2.90	3.91	4.47	4.56	4.69
(N)	(21)	(30)	(43)	(76)	(79)	(79)	(69)	(58)

This disjuncture between the rates of growth of mean military expenditure and GDP can be viewed in two ways. In what we term in Table 1.2 'Mean military expenditure as a percentage of Mean GDP', we in effect see the proportion of total Third World military expenditure to total GDP. In 'Mean (military expenditure as a percentage of GDP)' we see an average of the proportion of GDP allocated by each country to its military.[10] The first of these two measures is sensitive to the influence of larger countries, while the second gives equal weight to each country irrespective of its size. By either measure there is clearly an increase over time in the proportion of GDP devoted to the military. In particular, we may note from the second measure that an increasing proportion of Third World countries are committing an increasing proportion of their GDP to the military.[11]

This change is the exact obverse of the NATO countries, where there has been a general decline over the postwar period in the proportion of GDP devoted to the military.[12] Though Third World countries have as yet to reach, on average, the highest point achieved by the NATO countries, the respective growth and decline paths of these two groups of countries crossed in 1970 since which time Third World countries have consistently committed a greater proportion of their GDP to the military.

Point 3

There is, not surprisingly, enormous variation across Third World countries in their absolute levels of military expenditure. This variation is positively skewed, according neatly thereby with a hierarchical model. Not at all so obviously, however, relative military expenditure also displays extensive variation

Thus far we have dealt primarily with Third World countries as an aggregated whole. In this and the subsequent section, we continue to develop our descriptive profile by disaggregating Third World countries' military expenditure to examine the degree of variation across them, focusing firstly on absolute levels of military expenditure.

Third World countries vary enormously in their levels of military expenditure. In 1982, for example, they range from Sierre Leone expending $6 m to Saudi Arabia expending $15,759 m (in constant 1975 $). This variation, as we may note from the standard deviations of Table 1.3, is strongly positively skewed, meaning that as we go up the scale of values of military expenditure we find fewer countries. We see, in other words, a hierarchical organization of military capabilities. We may also note from Table 1.3 that the ratio of standard deviations to mean values increases over time, indicating that the hierarchy is getting progressively more stretched out.

Table 1.3: Means and standard deviations of military expenditure and percentage military expenditure in unlogged and logged values, selected years 1954–82

| | Military expenditure | | | | | % Military expenditure | | | | |
| | Unlogged | | Logged | | | Unlogged | | Logged | | |
	Mean	Standard deviation	Mean	Standard deviation	(N)	Mean	Standard deviation	Mean	Standard deviation	(N)
1954	178	229	1.93	0.59	25	2.5	1.8	0.30	0.30	21
1958	199	255	1.96	0.60	36	3.2	2.5	0.39	0.31	33
1962	153	250	1.68	0.74	61	2.9	3.0	0.30	0.36	61
1966	188	344	1.72	0.74	76	3.0	3.1	0.32	0.35	76
1970	269	463	1.85	0.76	79	3.9	4.6	0.39	0.40	81
1974	443	927	1.97	0.80	80	4.1	5.7	0.38	0.41	83
1978	597	1217	2.14	0.78	76	4.7	5.2	0.47	0.41	79
1982	846	2160	2.28	0.80	58	4.7	4.9	0.49	0.40	60

Such positive skewing is likely to be troublesome for analysis, especially when other variables to be associated with military expenditure are also skewed (which they are). Consequently, it is appropriate to make a log transformation (we use common logs). This, as again we see from Table 1.3, has the effect of producing pleasantly normal distributions.

Other things being equal, we would expect substantial variation across Third World countries if for no other reason than that they vary enormously in terms of size, whether size be measured by population, territory or GDP. Many Third World countries could not even begin to approximate in their gross military expenditure the levels of the largest spenders. For example, if Sierre Leone committed, impossibly, every dollar of its GDP to the military, it would still achieve a military expenditure of just over 3 per cent that of Saudi Arabia.

Using GDP to control for size, we still find substantial variation in relative military expenditure. This again has a tendency to positive skewing, albeit not as chronically as in the case of absolute military expenditure. Again log transformations eradicate the skewing and produce nicely normal distributions. The extent of the variation may be assessed by noting that in 1982, for example, a 95 per cent confidence interval gives a range of countries lying at one-sixth of to six times the mean value.

This variation may be put into perspective by comparing Third World with NATO countries. While NATO countries also display enormous variation in absolute expenditure levels, sufficient as we have argued above to posit a two-tier model, they display markedly less variation in relative commitment to military expenditure.[13]

Absolute military expenditure in Third World countries is expectedly extremely varied and as such stacks Third World states in a rather extended hierarchy. Not nearly so obviously, Third World states manifest substantial heterogeneity in their relative commitments to military expenditure.

Point 4

Overwhelmingly Third World countries expand their military expenditure over time, and for the most part do so in a relatively stable manner. It would be erroneous, however, to think of Third World military expenditure as a homogeneously expanding phenomenon. Not only are rates of growth of both absolute and relative military expenditure extremely variable, but the latter even show some significant contraction for a sizeable number of countries. There are no signs of convergence or any emergent norm for Third World military spending. In fact Third World countries manifest increasingly diverse commitments to the military

We have already seen that mean military expenditure for Third World countries increases according to a constant proportionate growth. While this would lead us to expect that a majority of countries would show a positive increase, it does not tell us anything about the variability across countries. To discover this, we need to consider the regressions of military expenditure over time for each Third World country.

These regressions show that an overwhelming majority of Third World countries, just under 90 per cent, experience significant proportionate increases in their military expenditure.[14] The R^2 measure from each regression can now be used to tell us something about the relative stability of growth. Were a country not to deviate from a proportionate growth path, irrespective of the actual value of the rate of growth, then we would find an R^2 of 1.00. Reductions from 1.00, assuming no better model could be fitted, would indicate increasing oscillations.[15] Excluding those cases for which we cannot produce a significant proportionate fit, we find the remaining cases have a mean R^2 value of 0.80. In other words, the overwhelming majority of Third World countries not only have a positive proportionate rate of growth in their military expenditure but a rate of growth which is relatively stable.

While this indicates an important commonality, it would be erroneous to leave this commonality unqualified. The first important qualification concerns the variation in the proportionate rates of growth of Third World countries which proves to be substantial. The distribution of rates of growth is approximately normal with a mean value and standard deviation respectively of 7.63 and 5.13.[16] This is a high standard deviation score relative to the mean value, which can be put into perspective by noting that two countries at plus and minus one standard deviation would have doubling times for their military expenditures of 6 and 29 years respectively. In this respect, some Third World countries are displaying absolute commitments to military expenditure that are driving them apart at a fairly rapid rate.

A second qualification concerns the behaviour of relative military expenditure. If each country's rate of growth of military expenditure equalled that of its GDP, then relative military expenditure over time would be a constant. The hierarchy of countries defined by their levels of relative military expenditures would remain unchanged over time. As it happens the mean rate of growth of GDP is lower than of military expenditure – on average GDP doubles every 16 years compared with 10 for military expenditure.[17] If the ratio of these two rates of growth was equal for all countries, then the location of countries in the hierarchy would remain unchanged but the mean value for relative military expenditure would shift upwards. Countries could be represented as following upwardly sloping parallel lines as opposed to a horizontal parallel line representation under equal rates of growth of both military expenditure and GDP.

In reality, though rates of growth of military expenditure and GDP are positively correlated, the relationship is far from perfect.[18] Ratios of rates of growth of military expenditure and GDP are not only variable but greater and lesser than unity.[19] Roughly 60 per cent of countries show significant positive increases in relative military expenditure; 19 per cent show no significant change; while 21 per cent have significant negative decreases.[20] As opposed to models of horizontal or upwardly sloping parallel lines, we find criss-crossing lines moving in all directions. Importantly, while a focus on absolute military expenditure gives an impression of overwhelming, increasing commitment, albeit at very variable rates, a focus on relative military expenditure indicates that roughly one-fifth of countries are not expanding – while a further one-fifth are actually contracting their relative commitment.

There appears, furthermore, to be no emerging norm for relative military expenditure. A convergence hypothesis would anticipate different rates of growth but would predict an inverse relation between increments to relative military expenditure and mean relative military expenditure. Although this plot is not very pleasant, the sign for this relationship is positive rather than negative. Furthermore, we may recall from Table 1.3 that the coefficients of variation of relative military expenditure generally increase. In other words, differentials in relative commitment are if anything increasing, in which respect Third World military expenditure can be said to be somewhat volatile.

Point 5

For a majority of Third World countries, military expenditure appears to attract some special preference, indicative of its being designated a high-priority area

Not only is it the case, as we have already noted, that a majority of Third World countries expand their military expenditure more rapidly than their GDP, but also a paired t-test on these two rates of growth indicates that the rate of growth of military expenditure is significantly higher than that of GDP.[21]

The propensity for military expenditure to expand more rapidly than GDP, remembering that this is not universal, holds, furthermore, across the range of rates of growth of GDP. Thus, we tested whether those countries with lower rates of growth of GDP would be more inclined to have rates of growth of military expenditure below those of GDP. This would imply a kind of 'fair weather' hypothesis for military expansion, leading us to predict, for the regression of rates of growth of military expenditure on rates of growth of GDP, a negative intercept and a b coefficient greater than 1. In fact, the b coefficient is marginally greater than 1 but the intercept is comfortably positive.[22]

Thus, while the citizens of the overwhelming majority of Third World states have witnessed a sustained real growth of GDP, the citizens of smaller – though still a majority – number of states have also witnessed an increasing proportion of that growth being devoted to the military.[23] Furthermore, there are no signs that only those countries with higher rates of growth of GDP allow their military expenditure to grow at a faster rate than GDP, the 'fair-weather' hypothesis. Consequently, we infer that some special and fairly generalized priority is devoted to the military.[24]

Notes

1. For similar descriptive profiles, see: N. Ball, *Third World Security Expenditures: A Statistical Compendium* (Stockholm: Swedish National Defence Research Institute, 1983); N. Ball, 'Security Expenditure: Measurement and Trends', in S. Deger and R. West (eds), *Defense Security and Development* (London: Pinter, 1987); annual publications (as from 1958) of *World Armaments and Disarmament* (Stockholm International Peace Research Institute).
2. There are a number of problems with data on Third World military expenditure of which two in particular need to be noted. The first concerns sources and definitions. Ideally we would like to use figures collated and standardized by an intergovernmental organization. We cannot do this as no such compendium exists, though the United Nations has both tried and failed to achieve this task. Traditionally the major sources have been the International Institute for Strategic Studies, the Arms Control and Disarmament Agency of the US government and the Stockholm International Peace Research Institute (SIPRI). Of these three sources the latter two are more reliable and extensive in their coverage. We use SIPRI data principally because latterly SIPRI has adopted a definition and figures that come largely from the International Monetary

Fund, *Government Financial Statistical Yearbook* (in other words the closest we can get to an ideal). Though there are unquestionably some remaining difficulties, we do have reasonably reliable figures. For a full definition of what constitutes military expenditure, see any recent annual publication of *World Armaments and Disarmament*. For a discussion of problems associated with various sources, see Ball, 'Security Expenditure: Measurement and Trends', op. cit. The second problem concerns valuation of military expenditure. We have taken SIPRI and IMF currency values which have been translated into constant prices using a cost-of-living index based on 1975 (which we have computed from IMF, *International Financial Statistics*) and transformed into dollars at a 1975 exchange rate. This traditional method of achieving constant dollar values, essential for longitudinal and cross-sectional comparison, does have some difficulties but is superior in our view to any other current alternative. For a discussion of an alternative strategy using purchasing power parities, see: R.L. West, 'Improved Measures of the Defence Burden in Developing Countries', in S. Deger and R. West (eds), op. cit. For a critical evaluation of purchasing power parities, see: R. Marris, 'Comparing the Incomes of Nations', *Journal of Economic Literature*, 22, 1984.

3. The figures for Table 1.1 are taken from SIPRI Yearbooks, whereas normally we use our own constant dollar transformations, as explained above, from SIPRI current local currency values. To make the figures in Table 1.1 comparable with the rest of the text, the heading 'Third World' has been adjusted to include those countries constituting our project population.

4. We might note something of an imbalance between the allies of the United States and those of the Soviet Union. In the case of the latter, their combined expenditure in 1985 constitutes 2.1 per cent of the world total, whereas the respective figure for the former is 18.5 per cent.

5. These include Saudi Arabia, Iran, Iraq, Israel, Egypt, Syria, Libya, Indonesia, India, Pakistan, South Korea, Taiwan, Thailand, South Africa, Argentina, Brazil and Chile.

6. See for example: M. Brzoska and T. Ohlson (eds), *Arms Production in the Third World* (London: Taylor and Francis, 1986); and M. Brzoska and T. Ohlson, *Arms Transfers to the Third World* (Oxford: Oxford University Press, 1987).

7. A focus on the mean level is useful in that we can now in effect control for the number of countries that are independent at any one time. It does not, however, totally alleviate our problem in that the countries being added to our population over time are not necessarily of randomly equal size. This difficulty will be overcome later.

8. The simple linear fit of military expenditure to time is also highly significant, with an R^2 value of 0.76. The linear fit would imply a constant absolute increase in volume of military expenditure over time, which in turn would mean a reducing proportionate increase. The regression of logged military expenditure on time gives an R^2 of 0.82. This equation is of the form $ME = 10^{a+bt}$. At t_1 $ME = 10^{a+b}$ and at t_2 $ME = 10^{a+2b}$. The proportionate change in ME from t_1 to t_2 is $(MEt_2 - MEt_1)/ME_{t1}$ or $(ME_{t2}/ME_{t1}) - 1$. Since $10^{a+2b} - 10^{a+b} = ME_{t2}/ME_{t1}$, then the antilog of the regression coefficient minus one yields a measure of the annual proportionate rate of growth.

9. The simple linear regression of mean GDP over time is highly significant with an R^2 of 0.75. Again the logged regression is not only easier to interpret but yields a better fit at R^2 of 0.83.

10. These two measures are respectively $(\geqslant ME / \geqslant GDP)/N$ and $\geqslant (ME/GDP)/N$.

11. The regression of this second measure over time yields an R^2 of 0.87 and the linear regression coefficient has a value of 0.08. In other words, roughly every twelve years Third World countries' mean relative military expenditure increases by 1 percentage

point. Clearly such a linear increase could not continue forever (though it would take over a thousand years to reach the absurd limit of relative military expenditure being equal to 100 per cent of GDP). More realistically we might expect relative military expenditure to follow a logistic curve, though there is as yet little sign of this.

12. The mean relative military expenditure figures for the NATO countries are: 4.3 (1950), 5.3 (1955), 4.5 (1960), 4.2 (1965), 3.9 (1970), 3.8 (1975), 3.4 (1980), 3.7 (1982).

13. The coefficient of variation for the NATO countries are: 0.40 (1950), 0.39 (1955), 0.43 (1960), 0.39 (1965), 0.48 (1970), 0.45 (1975), 0.46 (1980), 0.46 (1982).

14. Nine countries do not show significant positive equations: Afghanistan, Burma, Dominican Republic, Ghana, Guyana, Haiti, Niger, Uganda and Zaire. Of these, two, Ghana and Niger, have significant negative equations.

15. The R^2 value could reduce not because of oscillations but because we were fitting the wrong model. We have however tried alternative models and furthermore plots indicate that low R^2 values are indeed a function of oscillations rather than another model. The only model which could work would be a sine one, which in any event would be testimony to oscillation.

16. The distribution is in fact slightly positively skewed, which we may note from the mean and median values of 7.63 and 6.91. Furthermore, we have excluded one case, Libya, which has a very high value.

17. Again the overwhelming majority of countries have significant positive proportionate growth (all except Afghanistan, Ethiopia, Ghana, Guyana, Jamaica, Liberia, Tanzania, Uganda, Zaire and Zambia). Only one country, Zaire, has a significant negative growth. GDP growth is more stable than that of military expenditure. Excluding the insignificant cases, the mean R^2 value is 0.88 compared to the 0.80 for military expenditure. The distribution of rates of growth of GDP are approximately normal (mean and median values of 4.39 and 4.83 indicating a slight negative skewing) and again there is some substantial variation (standard deviation of 3.24).

18. The simple correlation is 0.43.

19. The rate of growth of military expenditure is lower than that of GDP in 26 per cent of cases.

20. The 19 per cent that achieve no significant change can do so either because relative military expenditure is constant or because it oscillates, though around a constant mean value. If we regard a case as oscillating if it has a coefficient of variation greater than 0.33, then in fact only 12 per cent of cases have a stable level of relative military expenditure.

21. To be on the conservative side, we have excluded Libya from this test on account of its very high value for the rate of growth of military expenditure. The difference in means between the two rates of growth is 3.37, which is significant beyond the 0.001 level.

22. Under the 'fair-weather' hypothesis, the b coefficient would have to be greater than 1 in order to produce a mean overall value for rate of growth of military expenditure higher than that for GDP. The regression in fact produces: rate of growth of military expenditure = 3.06 + 1.07 (rate of growth of GDP). This has an R^2 value of 0.34, significant beyond the 0.1 level.

23. Reversing the order of the variables leads to the issue of the effect of military expenditure on the performance of GDP. This issue is extremely complex and has yielded, from different studies, opposing and generally indecisive sets of results. See, for example: E. Benoit, *Defence and Economic Growth in Developing Countries* (Boston:

D.C. Heath, 1973); E. Benoit, 'Growth and Defence in Developing Countries', *Economic Development and Cultural Change*, 26, 1978; S. Deger and S. Sen, 'Military Expenditure, Spin-Off and Economic Development', *Journal of Development Economics*, 13, 1983; S. Deger and R.P. Smith, 'Military Expenditure and Growth in LDCs', *Journal of Conflict Resolution*, 27, 1983; S. Deger, 'Economic Development and Defence Expenditure', *Economic Development and Cultural Change*, 35, 1986; S. Deger and S. Sen, 'Defence, Entitlement and Development' in S. Deger and R. West (eds), op. cit; R. Fainzi, P. Arnez and L. Taylor, 'Defence Spending, Economic Structure and Growth', *Economic Development and Cultural Change*, 32, 1984. We note merely some simple, bivariate results. First, as we have already seen, higher rates of growth of military spending are most assuredly not associated with lower rates of growth of GDP. Second, higher levels of relative military spending do not predict to lower rates of growth of GDP. For this test we correlate the average level of relative military expenditure for each country over a four-year period with its rate of growth of GDP over the same years plus one. The results for the eight test periods (1950–4, 1954–8 etc. to 1978–82) yield one positive but seven insignificant results. The only positive result, furthermore, is for the period 1950–4, which is based on a rather small number of cases.

24. Point 5 as a whole is not only important but really begins to take us beyond the immediate concerns of a descriptive profile. As such it should be regarded as a transitional or bridging note, which is to be explored in much greater detail in the main body of the study.

2   Research Design

We have chosen to write this chapter in what we might call minimalist form. This is partly because any discussion of research design can run the danger of occupying a book in its own right. It is also because aspects of the research design are discussed throughout each of the following chapters and especially in the Conclusion. Consequently, at this stage, we intend to set out simply the bare outlines of what and how we hope to achieve.

Objectives

The subject matter of the military, with its ramifications for conflict, power and security, has been of understandably perennial interest to political scientists. So generalized is the importance of the military, however, that political scientists have never held a monopoly on the examination of the military. Economists, in particular, have made substantial contributions not only to more narrowly conceived economic facets of military behaviour but also to a more general understanding.[1] In fact the analysis of the military is ideally suited to cross-disciplinary research.

In the post-World War II period, political scientists have concentrated their attentions, eminently understandably in some respects, on the so-called strategic relationship of the superpowers and their allies.[2] With the exception of the phenomenon of military coups and regimes, picked up at an early stage by political scientists interested in development, the analysis of the Third World military has been a relatively neglected area. In the last few years, a number of attempts, particularly on the part of economists, have been made to rectify this relative neglect.[3]

The most general goal of this study is to contribute towards an understanding of what we take to be a relatively neglected but self-evidently important area of investigation, that of Third World military expenditure.[4] The principal objective of this study, following a broadly cross-disciplinary approach, is to identify the determinants of Third World military expenditure and to combine these determinants into a theory of military expenditure. More specifically, as a consequence of the descriptive profile of the preceding chapter, this theory must be capable of answering three main questions:

- why is there a seemingly ubiquitous commitment to the military;
- why is this commitment seemingly enduring;
- what accounts for the variability in military commitment across Third World countries.[5]

While the greater part of our efforts, in practical terms, is devoted to pursuing this first objective, a secondary objective is to explore the implications of Third World military expenditure. We would regard our principal objective as the vehicle by which we can produce empirically corroborated explanations of the behaviour of military expenditure. Our secondary objective, though decidedly less formalized than the analysis inherent in the first, is to complement and generalize upon an explanation of the determinants of military expenditure by considering the implications or inferences we may draw from a theory of military expenditure. Though clearly derivative on pursuit of our principal objective, we hope through our secondary objective to provide a more general understanding or appreciation of military expenditure.[6]

Method and format

Pursuit of our principal objective rests on the methods and goals of behavioural inquiry. We take behavioural inquiry to be a distinctive epistemology, characterized, independently of the substantive areas in which it is employed, by a set of assumptions and procedures designed to produce a particular type of knowledge. Behavioural research begins from the assumption that there are patterns or regularities in human behaviour and that such patterns are amenable to empirical description. Successful identification of such patterns defines the main object or focus for subsequent research. (It was precisely in such an endeavour in which we were engaged in the preceding chapter and it is from this investigation of descriptive patterns of military expenditure that we have derived our principal objective.) Patterns of behaviour, or systematic descriptions of variability, are not seen as random but as contingent on identifiable factors or explanations. Such explanations are arrived at through a process of controlled investigation, which in turn consists of a more particular set of techniques and a more general set of design procedures.

Having identified various patterns of behaviour, the goal of behavioural research is to employ controlled investigation to produce theories, or bodies of tested and interrelated hypotheses having explanatory content.[7] Our principal objective then is quite simply to apply the cannons of behavioural research to the substantive area of Third World military expenditure. In other words, having identified a number of regularities in military expenditure, we aim to test a series of explanations for these regularities.

This exercise is conducted across each of the succeeding chapters, apart from the final one. Each of these chapters, precisely because we are engaged in a standardized exercise, is written to an identical format.

The Introduction, the first section of each chapter, is devoted to specifying a general working hypothesis, the variables used to test this hypothesis, and a rationale that underpins the hypothesis. The general working hypothesis is simply a stipulation in operational or testable form of a relationship between a set of predictor variables and military expenditure. This relationship is based on or explained by the rationale. The rationale consists of a set of assumptions, which we take to be general statements which though empirical in form are often sufficiently generalized as to be difficult to test directly. These assumptions are designed to provide explanatory content for the hypotheses, which therefore are simply statements of testable relationships logically derived from the assumptions. The rationale, in other words, represents our attempt to provide a hopefully fairly generalized explanation as to why we would expect the relationships, profiled in the general working hypothesis, to hold.

The Findings, the second section of each chapter, is devoted primarily to a set of fairly standard tasks. It will contain a statement of the particular test procedures we employ.[8] It will contain a discussion of the results from the tests of the general working hypothesis. It will also contain an often fairly lengthy critical appraisal of these results, which may seem rather bizarre. This appraisal, however, is a crucial ingredient of behavioural research, as we construe it. The process of trying to find corroborated hypotheses is one which is fraught with many pitfalls. The critical appraisal constitutes our attempt to confront these pitfalls. In so doing it should become clear that our conceptualization of behavioural research is one founded much more in doubt and uncertainty rather than in truth or conclusive proof. Finally, there will be some discussion of the implications, following our second objective, we draw from our findings. This exercise becomes possible principally on account of the rationale. Had we worked simply on the basis of testing hypotheses for which we had not produced any explanatory content, then there would be little to discuss other than the relative success or failure of purely descriptive relationships. By virtue of building explanatory content into our hypotheses through the establishment of rationales, from which the hypotheses are derived, then we have the basis on which, so we hope, some interesting discussion of implications may be developed. In other words, the subject matter of the implications is defined by the content of the rationale.

The Summary, the final section of each chapter, contains no new information but represents a condensation of the main points of the Introduction and Findings.[9]

The following chapters differ, therefore, not in format, which includes design and objective as well as structure, but in substantive content. Each chapter may be thought of therefore as constituting a particular model of military expenditure.[10] The inclusion of multiple models is an important and very deliberate feature of the design of this study as a whole. We include multiple models, which have sometimes overlapping and sometimes quite different rationales, on three grounds. First, it is possible that the behaviour of military expenditure is multifaceted. Second, as we discuss more fully in the Conclusion, the failure of hypotheses, assuming there is a plausible rationale, is not only interesting but important. Third, a distinctive feature of the social sciences is that it is relatively easy to think up explanations. In general, the analysis of behaviour suffers rather more from a potential surfeit rather than a deficit of explanation, in which respect behaviour is over- as opposed to under-determined. As such, a major problem confronting behavioural analysis is not simply to find corroborated explanations but also to adjudicate between several possible explanations, all of which seemingly are corroborated.[11] A critically important feature of the overall design of this study consequently is that not only do we attempt to test several sets of explanations but these sets are tested against each other.[12]

The population of this study consists of all Third World countries, which we take to be those states which are not members of the major Western and Eastern blocs of the OECD or COMECON. The time frame for the study is 1950–82. 1950 represents a suitable starting point for the post-World War II period, while 1982 was the last year, at the time the data analysis began, for which we could collect extensive data. Countries are included from 1950 or their year of independence, if later than 1950, or the year from which data on that country became available.[13]

The data set on which the analysis is based is of the cross-national aggregate variety, where data has been taken from a number of standard courses. While unquestionably there must be reliability problems, the data is as reliable as we can find.[14]

Generally speaking the analysis is cross-sectional. Cross-sectional analysis can incur a number of problems as compared to time series analysis. On the other hand, times series analysis equally has a number of difficulties. We try to overcome the cross-sectional problems both by running our analysis at repeated intervals and by using some variables that explicitly measure change over time.[15]

The final chapter attempts to integrate the analysis conducted in the following six chapters. On the basis of the results of the main chapters it attempts to piece together a theory of military expenditure which can satisfactorily confront the questions of the ubiquity, enduring nature and variability in military commitment. This represents the culmination of our first objective. It also seeks, on grounds explained more fully at the time, to subject this theory to critical scrutiny. In so doing it augments but does not supplant, since it works on a different level, the discussion, which continues throughout all the main chapters, of the implications of military expenditure, our secondary objective.

Notes

1. A classic illustration can be seen for example in the work of Schelling: T.C. Schelling, *The Strategy of Conflict* (London: Oxford University Press, 1960); T.C. Schelling, *Arms and Influence* (New Haven: Yale University Press, 1966).
2. So extensive is this work that it has moved to 'textbook status'. For good examples, see: J. Baylis *et al.*, *Contemporary Strategy*, vols 1 and 2 (London: Croom Helm, 1987); B. Buzan, *An Introduction to Strategic Studies* (London: Macmillan, 1987).

3. So recent in fact is much of this work that it has appeared in print during the lifetime of this project. See for example: E. Benoit, *Defence and Economic Growth in Developing Countries* (Lexington: D.C. Heath, 1973); S. Deger and S. Sen, 'Military Expenditure, Spin-Off and Economic Development', *Journal of Development Economics*, **13**, 1983; S. Deger and R.P. Smith, 'Military Expenditure and Growth in Less Developed Countries', *Journal of Conflict Resolution*, **27**, 2, 1983; S. Deger, 'Economic Development and Defence Expenditure', *Economic Development and Cultural Change*, **35**, 1986; S. Deger, *Military Expenditure in Third World Countries: The Economic Effects* (London: Routledge, 1986); S. Deger and R.L. West (eds), *Defence, Security and Development* (London: Pinter, 1987); W.J. Dixon and B.E. Moon, 'The Military Burden and Basic Human Needs', *Journal of Conflict Resolution*, **30**, 1986; R. Fainzi, P. Annez and L. Taylor, 'Defence Spending, Economic Structure and Growth', *Economic Development and Cultural Change*, **32**, 3, 1984; P.C. Frederiksen and R.E. Looney, 'Defence Expenditures and Economic Growth in Developing Countries', *Armed Forces and Society*, **3**, 4, 1983; J.H. Lebovic and A. Ishaq, 'Military Burden, Security Needs and Economic Growth in the Middle East', *Journal of Conflict Resolution*, **31**, 1, 1987; D. Lim, 'Another Look at Growth and Defense in Less Developed Countries', *Economic Development and Cultural Change*, **31**, 2, 1983; R.E. Looney, 'Determinants of Military Expenditure in Developing Countries', *Arms Control*, **8**, 3, 1987; A. Maizels and M.K. Nissanke, 'The Determinants of Military Expenditure in Developing Countries', *Discussion Paper*, 85–18, University College, London, 1985, D.K. Whynes, *The Economics of Third World Military Expenditure* (London: Macmillan, 1979).

4. The dependent variables of this study are gross military expenditure, which we generally refer to as absolute military expenditure, and relative military expenditure, which is the gross measure as a percentage of GDP. Though these two measures are clearly related, a relationship which is all the more close as we see in the next chapter as we discover that GDP is a major predictor of absolute military expenditure, we use both measures as in principle they point to different facets. The absolute measure profiles what we term 'battlefield capabilities'. Thus, we assume for calculations in the context of power, security or conflict that it is the absolute size of military capabilities across states that is critical. Relative military expenditure is of course independent of size and as such provides a measure of what is often termed the military burden.

5. We see these questions as being interrelated rather than autonomous or discrete. Consequently, the answers to the questions must also be interrelated. The last of the three questions is in one critical respect the most demanding precisely because it deals in variability and as such requires the identification of factors which, though generalizable across a large number of cases, can also provide explanations for individual cases. Consequently, the bulk of our attention focuses on the third question, albeit subject to the requirement that a satisfactory answer in this context must be related to the answers we would produce for the first two rather more general questions.

6. It might reasonably be argued that the obvious flip-side to an examination of the determinants of military expenditure would be to analyse the consequences. Strictly speaking an examination of consequences would stipulate a number of potentially interesting and important areas, which in effect would become dependent variables, and look for the impact of military expenditure, now in effect an independent variable, on them. Much of the recent work by economists has in fact done this, taking economic development to be the consequence of interest. We are not concerned in our second

objective to focus on a particular consequence or set of consequences partly because this would entail another study in its own right, partly because we would face an almost endless list of possible consequences with no readily obvious means of selection, but mainly because we are concerned to look for rather more general implications rather than immediate consequences.

7. For fuller and now rather classic, though differing, discussions, see: P. Abell, *Model Building in Sociology* (London: Weidenfeld and Nicholson, 1971); J. Galtung, *Theory and Methods of Social Research* (London: Allen and Unwin, 1967); A. Kaplan, *The Conduct of Inquiry* (San Francisco: Chandler, 1964); F.N. Kerlinger, *Foundations of Behavioural Research* (New York: Holt, Rinehart and Winston, 1973); A.L. Stinchombe, *Constructing Social Theories* (New York: Harcourt, Brace and World, 1968); D. Willer, *Scientific Sociology* (Englewood Cliffs: Prentice-Hall, 1967).

8. Our main test procedure is multiple regression. Generally we use a stepwise format, though we also on occasion use forced entry. We favour the use of pairwise deletion to cope with missing data but also run listwise deletions and use the latter if mismatches develop. Residuals are tested throughout across an extensive battery of tests. Relatively high tolerance values are used to cope with multicollinearity problems. In tables we report b coefficients and in parentheses standardized beta values. Unless we state otherwise, all coefficients reported in tables are significant at the 0.05 level or higher.

9. In principle the Summary is entirely redundant. We have included such a section mainly because the discussion in the Findings can become both long and complex. We have, however, endeavoured to keep the discussion in the Findings as straightforward as possible by relegating much of the more technical discussion to footnotes.

10. By model we mean a set of predictor variables related to the dependent variable of military expenditure through the rationale.

11. A depressingly frequent approach in social-science investigation is to take a so-called theory, usually in this context a synonym for an argument, and look for supporting evidence. Should any such evidence be found, the theory is then held to be proved. Our point is not just that a theory is something which comes at the end rather than the beginning of analysis, nor just that we should search for falsifying evidence, but crucially that competing explanations need to be evaluated. In an area of overdetermined and often overlapping explanations, particularly when all explanations are probabilistic, it is a serious blunder not to force different explanations, that may have some corroboration, to compete against each other.

12. Though for the sake of simplicity and clarity of presentation we write up each chapter as a separate model, reserving to the Conclusion our final equations, this is not how we have conducted our analysis. The variables contained in any one model have constantly been tested alongside major variables from other models. There is no ideal strategy for producing the best set of variables from a large data set such as we employ. In our view we can rely to some extent on techniques such as stepwise procedures combined with non-statistical reasoning, as found in the rationales. All we can then do is to run large numbers of regressions to find robust predictors and use those alongside the variables contained in any one model. The kind of stages in which we present our discussion in Chapters 3–8 is then not a direct reflection of the chronology of our analysis but a simplified form to make for clearer presentation.

13. The list of countries included in the project together with their dates of inclusion is contained in an Appendix to this chapter.

14. The variables we employ and the data sources are provided in the relevant chapters.

All the gross variables of an economic variety are put into constant dollar prices, based of course on the same year. The overwhelming majority of our variables, other of course than dummy variables, are put into log form (we use common logs). The reasons for this are that scatterplots of the untransformed variables show substantial bunching at low values and a high degree of heteroscedasticity. The log transformations produce nicely normal distributions. Standardized beta values can be interpreted in exactly the same way as untransformed variables in multiple regression equations. The b coefficients should, however, be interpreted in terms of proportionate rather than absolute changes. Dummy variables in multiple regression equations have the same interpretation, though their value is of course added to the constant term. Log transformation create difficulties with zeros and negative scores. Generally speaking we transform zeros into low scores, such as 1 or 0.1 depending on scale. Generally, with negative scores, we take the log of the absolute value and then reinsert the sign.

15. Cross-sectional analysis can be especially awkward, and, under certain circumstances, decidedly misleading. This is especially true when we deal with time changes. It is possible, for example, to find positive associations between two variables at different time points even though over the two time points the relationship between the variables was negative. Time series analysis, however, can also have major problems of which low variation is probably the most awkward. In principle, the cross-sectional design better suits our purposes. Furthermore, by running repeated analyses and using some variables, such as rates of growth, to measure change we can overcome many of the dangers inherent in cross-sectional designs. We collect data on an annual basis for our overall data base. (Generally in the regressions the independent variables are lagged by one year on military expenditure.) For much of the analysis we use test years at four yearly intervals of 1954, 1958, 1962, 1966, 1970, 1974, 1978, 1982. These test years are sometimes referred to as two year files, i.e. independent variables measured on say 1953 and dependent on 1954. Sometimes, whenever we deal with change variables, we use five year files, e.g. independent variables are measured, say, 1950–53 and the dependent in 1954.

Appendix   Project Population by Year of Inclusion

Afghanistan	1964
Algeria	1963
Argentina	1950
Bangladesh	1973
Benin	1961
Bolivia	1955
Brazil	1950
Burma	1950
Burundi	1963
Cambodia	1959
Cameroon	1962
Central African Republic	1961
Chad	1961
Chile	1950
Colombia	1950

Congo	1963
Costa Rica	1950
Dominican Republic	1950
Ecuador	1950
Egypt	1954
El Salvador	1950
Ethiopia	1963
Gabon	1961
Ghana	1957
Guatemala	1950
Guyana	1966
Haiti	1955
Honduras	1950
India	1950
Indonesia	1951
Iran	1950
Iraq	1950
Israel	1950
Ivory Coast	1961
Jamaica	1963
Jordan	1950
Kenya	1964
South Korea	1953
Kuwait	1961
Lebanon	1950
Liberia	1963
Libya	1960
Madagascar	1960
Malawi	1965
Malaysia	1958
Mali	1961
Mauritania	1961
Mexico	1950
Morocco	1956
Nepal	1958
Nicaragua	1953
Niger	1961
Nigeria	1961
Oman	1960
Pakistan	1950
Panama	1950
Paraguay	1950
Peru	1950
Philippines	1950
Rwanda	1963
Saudi Arabia	1960
Senegal	1961
Sierra Leone	1961
Singapore	1966

Somalia	1961
South Africa	1950
Sri Lanka	1950
Sudan	1956
Syria	1950
Taiwan	1951
Tanzania	1962
Thailand	1955
Togo	1960
Tunisia	1956
Uganda	1963
United Arab Emirates	1972
Upper Volta	1961
Uruguay	1955
Venezuela	1950
South Vietnam	1958
Yemen Arab Republic	1969
Yemen Peoples Democratic Republic	1969
Zaire	1963
Zambia	1965
Zimbabwe	1966

3 Military Expenditure and Power Capabilities

Introduction

Before outlining the general working hypothesis of this chapter, we indicate briefly how we conceptualize power. Power we take to pertain to those capabilities, or resources, that may be used to affect the behaviour of others through threat or the infliction of deprivation. As such we conceptualize power in terms of means, as opposed to outcomes, which have some, albeit variable, coercive content.[1]

Taking military expenditure to constitute a key power capability, the main objective of this chapter is to explore the relationship between military expenditure and a number of other major power capabilities. The general working hypothesis states that a number of such main capabilities will predict positively to military expenditure. Within this general hypothesis, we are specifically interested in the extent to which power capabilities cohere and the degree to which military expenditure could be said to be determined by any of these other capabilities.

The rationale for this hypothesis rests, first and foremost, on the assumption that power is a critical predictor of control.[2] Control pertains to outcomes or more particularly to the successful use of the means of power or influence manifested when one party can cause another to take an action it would otherwise not have taken. Power or capabilities certainly do not represent the only variables of which account must be taken to predict to control. A comprehensive attempt to explain control would additionally have to consider intent and willingness to mobilize and use capabilities, appropriateness of capabilities, and constraints on the use of capabilities.[3]

From this we assume, furthermore, that states have a substantial incentive to maintain and promote their capabilities. Capabilities become most meaningful in a comparative or distributional context when, in other words, the capabilities of any one state are juxtaposed against those of other states. Comparing states in this manner produces then a ranking or hierarchy of states, within which the location of a state is of substantial importance. Other things being equal, higher location in this hierarchy, a direct reflection of magnitude of capabilities, will enhance the prospects of autonomy of a state and increase the margins of safety within which it can move. Thus, again other things being equal, more powerful states have greater capacity to control less powerful ones and conversely are less prone in turn to be controlled. Furthermore, and equally if not more importantly, more powerful states can set the rules or parameters within which state interaction takes place. Consequently, states have substantial incentives to maintain and develop their capabilities not as ends in themselves but as means to promote their position within the hierarchy thereby preserving their prospects of autonomy and margins of safety.

Finally, we assume there is a strong propensity for capabilities to cohere essentially because states create what we might call a reciprocating dynamic. Thus, while states, in some respects, can differ substantially, the salience of protecting autonomy and preserving margins of safety is such that it imposes a strong commonality on all states. As long as any one state wishes to compete in the hierarchy then it must promote the same range of capabilities as other states. Furthermore, although all capabilities can provide means to control capacities, different capabilities may be suitable to different circumstances. Since the international environment is one of substantial ambiguity and uncertainty, then no state can be sure of exactly which circumstances it is likely to face at any one time. Consequently, it is in the general security interests of any state to ensure that it maintains a broad range of capabilities so as to be prepared to meet all possible contingencies. In these respects, therefore, states in an environment characterized substantially, though not exclusively, by self-help create a dynamic, which is reciprocal in being based on mutual competition, that encourages the maintenance of a common and broad range of capabilities.

To test the general working hypothesis, we focus on a number of fairly standard capabilities, distinguished both in terms of the type of resource they profile and the form of measurement, which may be either absolute or relative (where by relative we mean that there is some control for size).

As far as absolute capabilities are concerned, we include: population size, perhaps the simplest and most traditional indicator; gross domestic product (GDP), the single most important measure of overall economic capability; exports, again an economic capability but one that taps more directly an international element; international liquidity, which provides a measure of economic strength reflecting the balance on a country's international transactions; and the number of embassies accredited to other states, which we take to reflect diplomatic status.[4] The relative capabilities consist of a set of economic variables which broadly speaking profile relative wealth. They include: per capita GDP; gross domestic fixed capital formation (GDFCF) as a percentage of GDP; industrial production as a percentage of GDP; international liquidity as a percentage of imports; and a number of rates of growth of key economic variables.[5]

Findings

Our first area of interest centres on the issue of the extent to which power capabilities cohere. As we see from Table 3.1, there is in general a marked degree of coherence among the absolute capabilities. Countries with larger GDPs also

Table 3.1: Correlation matrix for absolute capabilities, 1978

	ME	GDP	POP	IL	E
GDP	0.86	—	—	—	—
POP	0.59	0.73	—	—	—
IL	0.85	0.84	0.53	—	—
E	0.87	0.91	0.48	0.84	—
EMBTOT	0.70	0.74	0.56	0.62	0.66

tend to have larger volumes of trade, greater reserves, more diplomatic associations and larger militaries. This coherence furthermore is relatively stable over time.[6] Though no one capability is perfectly replicated by any other, the international power structure is massively more uni- as opposed to multi-dimensional.

There are, however, some variations in the strengths of association among the capabilities. Consequently, the regression results contained in Table 3.2 show GDP to be the single best predictor of military expenditure, though international economic capabilities appear to play an increasingly important role.

Table 3.2: Regression results of military expenditure on absolute capabilities, selected years 1954–82

Year	Coefficients	R^2
1954	0.97 (GDP)	0.75
1958	0.97(GDP)	0.70
1962	1.14(GDP)	0.78
1966	1.18(GDP)	0.81
1970	1.15(GDP)	0.76
1974	0.69(GDP) + 0.46(E) (0.53) (0.37)	0.78
1978	0.60(E) + 0.39(IL) (0.52) (0.41)	0.80
1982	0.64(GDP) + 0.37(IL) (0.53) (0.40)	0.80

We reserve until the next chapter a more detailed discussion of the international economic variables. Before turning to what we take the principal task to be, an exploration of the relationship of GDP to military expenditure, we note points on the relationships of diplomatic associations and population size.

We would not expect diplomatic associations to play a role as a causal influence on military expenditure and indeed have included it here for associational purposes. Commonly the use of force is juxtaposed against an alternative form of management in the guise of diplomacy. The strength of association between diplomatic ties and military expenditure is such that states, though no doubt aware of the distinction between force and diplomacy, clearly do not regard diplomatic associations and military expenditure as substitutes.

We may well have expected some causal link from population to military expenditure on the grounds that the military would exist in order to protect a particular population. The decidedly better predictive capacity of GDP points to military expenditure being more a function of what a state can afford than of the size of population that needs to be defended. This we would not regard as being inconsistent with a power perspective on the grounds that population size is increasingly of secondary rather than primary importance. For example, technology has transformed the means of force such that, other things being equal, quality and quantity of firepower is more important than human power.[7]

Turning to our second question, the extent to which any capability might be said to determine military expenditure, the most promising candidate would seem to be GDP. Although there is no reason to suppose that a power perspective would require any determinacy from GDP to military expenditure (it would require only strong association), an exploration of the possibility of a causal link does yield, in our view, some interesting insights.

The first of three connections we consider is what we might call a uniform carrying capacity. The reasoning here is that GDP defines the level of military expenditure to which any state may commit itself (hence the notion of a carrying capacity) and does this in a uniform manner across states. If this happened then relative military expenditure across states would be a constant. Such a position could be regarded as rational and conducive to security on a variety of grounds. No state could be said to be more aggressive than others by virtue of being seen to be willing to commit relatively greater resources to the military; competitive arms racing of the form where states bid up levels of relative military expenditure would not exist as all states would in effect be conforming to a globally diffused norm; or, in an area where states enjoyed greater volition (it is much easier to change military expenditure than GDP), states would be seen to be refraining from disturbing a status quo defined by the much less easily manipulated GDP. However, as we saw in Chapter 1, relative military expenditure is rather highly variable.[8]

This variability yields in fact a rather uncomfortable difficulty for the power capability perspective as we have outlined it. It means that there is some degree of misfit between GDP and military hierarchies. In other words, some states are committing substantially fewer resources to the military than others and thereby not maintaining, as we would expect, their location in an international military hierarchy.

The way in which this difficulty could be removed would be to find an explanation, consonant with power capability thinking, that could systematically account for this uncomfortable variation. One possibility is our second determinacy effect from GDP to military expenditure, which we label a variable carrying capacity.

The variable carrying capacity comes in two variants. By the first, military expenditure would proportionately reduce with increases in GDP. This would indicate that smaller states committed relatively greater resources to the military and in so doing would be compensating to some extent for their inferior position in the GDP hierarchy. Under the second variant, military expenditure would increase proportionately with GDP, indicating that larger states were using their military expenditure, which is generally speaking more malleable than GDP, to enhance their positions.[9]

Neither variant can be corroborated, which in turn means that we have a continuing difficulty with the power capability explanation.[10] It may be, of course, that there is a real problem in the power perspective reasoning. Consequently, our third attempt to establish a determinacy relation lies outside the power perspective framework.

It focuses on a more direct and explicitly economic explanation, profiled in terms of levels of development and performance. Under the first of two variants, relative military expenditure would increase with per capita income. We have already commented in the context of noting the stronger relationship to military expenditure of GDP, as compared with population size, that military expenditure appears to be more a function of what a country can afford than the size of the population to be defended. If relative military expenditure did increase with per capita income, plausible in the context of higher per capita income indicating a greater capacity to commit more resources to the military, then we would be seeing a greater marginal propensity to consume military goods as a function of rising income. This would indicate to us that military expenditure contained substantial 'luxury goods' connotations. There is, however, no corroboration for this variant.[11]

Under the second variant, we look for a positive relationship between rates of growth of per capita income and levels of relative military expenditure. Instead of seeing wealthier countries committing more resources, the 'luxury good' interpretation, we would be looking to see whether countries displaying better rates of growth, irrespective of income level, committed greater resources. If this were to be the case then military expenditure in part would be a function of economic performance or what we term a 'fair-weather' explanation. There is again, however, no corroboration for this variant.[12]

Summary

The primary objective of this chapter has been to explore military expenditure from a power capability perspective. The rationale posits that power capabilities are crucial predictors of a control capacity and that states have substantial incentives to develop capabilities principally because capabilities are critical in defining the structure of the international system and because they are vital to states as states strive to promote and protect their autonomy and margins of safety. Furthermore, on the grounds of what we have termed a reciprocating dynamic, we would expect capabilities to cohere. Under this rationale military expenditure becomes a function of the combination of the perceived importance of power capabilities and a view of a systemic arrangement of the international system, in which considerations of power, autonomy, security and hierarchy are prevalent.

There does seem to be some substantial corroboration for the general working hypothesis and the rationale on which it is based. In absolute terms power capabilities do cohere to a powerful extent, in which respect a hierarchy drawn in terms of any capability would be broadly replicated by any other capability.

The corroboration is also, however, far from perfect. The major difficulty is that while the international power system is most assuredly not multidimensional, it is not as closely unidimensional as we might expect. This is seen in particular when we examine the variability in relative military expenditure, discussed in the context of the failure of the uniform carrying capacity explanation. Some states clearly do not maintain a location in the military hierarchy consonant with their GDP, while other states equally surpass an expected location. Furthermore, an initial attempt to develop a systematic explanation of such under- and over-achieving in terms that are consonant with a power capability perspective, in the form of the variable carrying capacity explanation, does not succeed. Finally, the variation in absolute size across countries is such that it does tend to produce a strain away from multidimensionality. Thus, while it would be wrong to think that the coherence in absolute capabilities is spurious or artificial, the size variation does more or less automatically underwrite some movement toward some degree of coherence.

On the other hand, we can find no corroboration for a readily available alternative explanation which seeks to account for the troublesome unexplained variation of the under- and over-achievers in terms of levels of development or economic performance. The 'luxury good' and 'fair-weather' explanations, neither of which would concur comfortably with a power capabilities perspective, can be quite firmly rejected.

In sum, therefore, an explanation of the behaviour of military expenditure, couched in power capabilities reasoning, has some corroboration. This explanation is, however, not only partial but also we must entertain some doubts about its validity until such time as we can provide some systematic explanation of the variation in relative military expenditure which is compatible with power capability reasoning.

Notes

1. For fuller discussions see, for example: H. Sprout and M. Sprout, *Foundations of National Power* (New York: Van Nostrand, 1951); K.N. Waltz, *Theory of International Politics* (Reading: Addison, 1979).

2. Power is not the only route to control but rather coexists with influence which is conventionally held to rely less on the threat or use of coercion and more on the rather more positive promise of grants or benefits. In practice the distinction can often become blurred. Thus, for example, the effectiveness of diplomacy, commonly seen as a use of influence rather than power, may rest ultimately on coercive potential. For fuller and classic discussions, see, for instance: H.D. Lasswell and A. Kaplan, *Power and Society* (New Haven: Yale University Press, 1950); A. Wolfers, *Discord and Collaboration* (Baltimore: Johns Hopkins Press, 1962).

3. The more conventional definition generally speaking follows some variant of Dahl's, where power is seen as the ability on the part of A to get B to do something B otherwise would not have done. (See R.A. Dahl, 'The Concept of Power', *Behavioral Science*, 2, 1957.) We are inclined to agree with the discussion in Waltz, op. cit., that it is easier to separate means from outcomes, principally on the grounds that several relatively distinct sets of factors, of which means is one, explain outcomes. As long as it is remembered that power as means does not directly equate with power as outcome, then our variation from the more conventional definition is largely semantic as power as outcome is equated by us with control.

4. Data for these variables are taken from International Monetary Fund, *Financial Statistics*, except for industrial production, which is taken from United Nations, *Yearbook of National Account Statistics*.

5. Rates of growth, which can be interpreted as performance capabilities, are computed for per capita GDP, exports (in absolute and relative form) and international liquidity (in absolute and relative form). These have been computed over the four-year period prior to the military expenditure.

6. The correlation matrices for the other test years are very similar, and all show simple correlations significant way beyond the 0.05 level. The acronyms in Table 3.1 are: GDP (gross domestic product), POP (populations size), IL (international liquidity holdings), E (exports), EMBTOT (total number of embassies accredited to other states).

7. Curiously, were international management to rely extensively on intergovernmental organizations functioning pre-eminently, as do Western liberal democracies, on the basis of one person one vote, then population size would immediately become a terribly important capability. However, apart from the fact that intergovernmental organizations are often bypassed, voting rights in them are often determined, as in the case of the World Bank or International Monetary Fund, by economic capabilities. When these are not used and voting is based on one state one vote, as for instance in the United Nations General Assembly, then we commonly find a controlling 'corrective' mechanism, as for example in the Security Council. Generally speaking, Third World countries would benefit enormously if control through population size became an accepted international principle. We in fact learn something rather important about the international power structure by noting that high-income countries studiously avoid ceding control internationally to a mechanism, universal suffrage, to which domestically they attach considerable importance.

8. Another way of putting this test would be to require that logged regressions of military expenditure on GDP would produce R^2 values close to 1.00 and b coefficients close to unity. Though Table 3.2 shows that the coefficients are close to unity they are not sufficiently close, nor are the R^2 values sufficiently close to 1.00. It may seem strange, however, that a highly significant correlation between GDP and military expenditure yields such great variation in relative military expenditure. The main reason for this

(apart from the facts that the R^2 values are not 1.00 and the b coefficients are not unity) pertains to the enormous variation in size across countries. Thus, a larger state may expend at a much lower relative level than a smaller state but because of the great variation in GDP size the larger state absolutely would still be expending at a much higher level than the smaller state. Consequently we can obtain highly significant simple correlations between absolute variables but still find substantial variation in relative military expenditure.

9. Both the uniform and variable carrying capacities deal with what we would regard as strong carrying capacity effects, hence the reasoning in terms of determinacy. GDP does, of course, have a weak carrying capacity effect in that for all states it sets the final limits to which military expenditure can go. This weak effect, however, cannot be said to constitute either an interesting or strong determinacy effects.

10. These two variants would both require an R^2 value close to 1.00 from a regression of military expenditure on GDP but would then respectively require b coefficients smaller than or greater than unity. Putting this another way we would expect respectively that relative military expenditure would be either negatively or positive associated with GDP. Results show that the b coefficients are too close to unity and concomitantly regressions of relative military expenditure on GDP show GDP to be an insignificant estimator. While this determinacy effect could tolerate, indeed would require unlike the first effect, variation in relative military expenditure, it would also seek to explain that variation in terms of GDP. In fact we find that larger and smaller states, as defined by GDP, are equally prone to have higher or lower relative military expenditure scores.

11. We should expect to find significant correlations between relative military expenditure and per capita income (or what comes to the same thing, the regressions of gross military expenditure on the absolute capabilities should show both GDP and population to be significant estimators). There is in fact only one significant correlation in any of our test years, 1954, and that is negative. In the light of the smaller number of cases in 1954 and the subsequent correlations we pay no attention to this. The other correlations are 0.11 (1982), 0.18 (1978), 0.12 (1974), 0.11 (1970), 0.11 (1966), 0.09 (1962), and –0.19 (1958).

12. We should expect to find significant correlations between rate of growth of per capita income and relative military expenditure. The only significant correlation appears again in 1954 and again we pay no attention to this isolated result. The other correlations are 0.07 (1982), –0.13 (1978), –0.16 (1974), 0.01 (1970), 0.01 (1966), 0.01 (1962), 0.05 (1958). We even model an interactive effect, which would yield rather a weak interpretation in that a determinacy effect would be felt only with the simultaneous appearance of high income level and high performance, but this yields nothing. The other rates of growth also show no significant results. In fact the regressions of relative military expenditure on all the relative capabilities (which can all be regarded as some measure of development) and the rates of growth yield virtually nothing.

4 Military Expenditure and Budgetary Behaviour

Introduction

The objective of the last chapter was to explore the nature and behaviour of military expenditure by approaching it from the perspective of power capabilities and the notion of an international power hierarchy. The general objective of this chapter remains the same, in that we are concerned to amplify an understanding of military expenditure, but in this instance by approaching it from a budgetary perspective. In principal, at least, a budgetary perspective contains a number of important considerations not only and perhaps most obviously in the financial implications inherent in budgeting but also in that the budget profiles intent or commitment in the areas of political choice and control.

Certainly as far as high-income countries are concerned, the analysis of budgetary behaviour has rightly for a number of reasons become a major and enduring area of investigation. In the first place, the fiscal control inherent in budgets represents an extremely important instrument of macro-economic management.[1] While it is mainly economists who have examined budgets from the perspective of the impact of budgets on both domestic and international economic performance, political scientists have focused on budgets more from the perspective of political control.[2] Though it would be erroneous to regard budgets as being the sole or even principal means of governmental control, a second source of importance of the general subject area of budgeting is the argument that the magnitude of budget size is such that it is taken, and rightly so in our view, to indicate increasing state control, a subject we take to be of self-evident importance. A third major attraction of budget studies is that they provide a rich insight into governmental choice. Governments can and do raise revenue and expend it not only across a variety of different areas but also to varying degrees within these areas. Though no government can ever approach a budget in a *tabula rasa* fashion, to which extent it would be erroneous to take a budget profile as an unadulterated measure of a government's set of choices, nonetheless sufficient latitude remains that budgetary structure provides an important insight into a government's preferences and priorities.[3]

Although Third World budgets have not been subjected to anything like the systematic and extensive analysis of OECD country budgets, such is the generally accepted importance of budgets that Third World budgets most certainly have not gone unnoticed. Generally speaking, however, Third World budgets have attracted the attention of economic developmentalists rather than political scientists and the focus of the former has rested heavily on a set of conflicting and sometimes mutually contradictory exhortation as to how Third World countries should structure their budgets.

Thus writers such as Bauer or Johnson, reflecting market economy persuasions, emphasize the distinction between competition and government control arguing that it is only the former that provides an avenue for growth. Consequently Third World countries should set lower ceilings on budgetary expenditure and intervention.[4] While holding strongly to market principles, some other writers, such as Krauss for example, have argued that Third World countries do confront some distinctive problems which necessitate some adjustment to a pure competition model. For Krauss this should take the form of the 'competitive growth state', a model which does anticipate explicit governmental intervention, though critically intervention directly geared to the growth of the private economy.[5] Writers, reflecting more a democratic socialist than a liberal tradition, have on the other hand urged a more interventionist and expansive role for government. Development, it is argued, is not something which can be left to market forces but particularly in the context of late nation-state development needs to be orchestrated, controlled and promoted by central governments.[6] Yet another group of writers argue that the environment in which Third World countries find themselves is so radically different from that of Western countries that budgetary lessons from the latter are highly inappropriate for the former. Third World states consequently must develop new and distinctive forms of budgeting geared explicitly to their own needs.[7]

While these illustrations are not intended to be exhaustive, they are sufficient to illustrate that the issue of the budget is subject not only to controversy but to controversy of some considerable importance. As such there is common agreement that the size and structure of budgets are of major significance pre-eminently because the budget is held to be so crucial for economic and political development. Controversy over the size and structure of budgets is a function of the conflict over the ends to which political and economic development should be geared.

Leaving the exhortations to one side, we may consider the general descriptive form of Third World budgetary change. There has been not only a marked propensity for Third World budgets to expand but to expand more rapidly than GDP. Some 80 per cent of Third World countries display a significant positive linear rate of growth of their relative budget size (their budget as a percentage of GDP) over time.[8] This growth furthermore has carried budget size to quite high levels. As we see from Table 4.1, the mean Third World budget accounts for just over 10 per cent of GDP in 1950 but for nearly 30 per cent by 1982. Consequently, though there is unquestionably variation both in rates of growth and in size of budget across Third World countries, we may observe that budgetary expansion is a fairly generalized phenomenon across the Third World.[9]

This growth can be placed in perspective by comparing it with that of the OECD countries. In the post-World War II period the OECD countries also have followed a path of budgetary growth in excess of their GDP growth.[10]

Table 4.1: Mean and standard deviation of Third World budgets
as a percentage of GDP, selected years 1950–82

	1950	1954	1958	1962	1966	1970	1974	1978	1982
Mean	11.5	13.0	15.3	16.2	18.6	20.9	23.5	26.6	28.9
Standard deviation	6.3	4.9	6.7	7.3	7.5	9.4	12.2	13.3	13.9
N	14	21	27	34	55	64	72	70	50

Although relative budget size is higher on average in the OECD countries than in the Third World, a striking feature of Third World relative budget size is that it does not lag far behind that of the OECD countries. This lag in fact is substantially less than the per capita income differential across these two groups of countries, which means that Third World states maintain substantially higher budgets than the OECD countries did at analagous levels of development.[11]

In comparative historical terms, therefore, Third World budgets are on average very large, with Third World states attaching an importance or priority to budgets well beyond that of the high-income countries at equivalent levels of development. This high priority attached to budgets is a function, we suspect, of either or both of two main reasons. First, it could be reflective of Third World governments wishing to play an enhanced development or welfare role. Second, it could indicate a high-level appreciation on the part of Third World governments that the budget can be used as an instrument either to consolidate the general governmental apparatus or as a mechanism for fostering the support of particular groups.

Against this background we are interested to explore three particular sets of relationships between military expenditure and the budget. The first of these concerns the overall size of the budget, where we hypothesize that budget size, other things being equal, predicts positively to military expenditure. The immediate grounds for hypothesizing this relationship are that military expenditure may increase with budget size either because the military simply becomes a beneficiary of larger public spending or because the military is expanded as part of the central government's drive to consolidate its control.

Budget accounts provide useful insights into some of the financial constraints facing governments. The second focus examines the relationship between these constraints and military expenditure, where assuming financial constraints restrict a government's expenditure latitude, other things being equal, we hypothesize an inverse relationship between military expenditure and such constraints.

The third and final set of relationships to be explored focuses on the link between military expenditure and health and education expenditure. Budgetary expenditures unquestionably to some degree reflect governments' preferences and priorities. Though present-day governments expend across a staggeringly similar set of areas, they can attach diffe rent priorities to those areas. At some level an expenditure in any one area incurs an opportunity cost in another, assuming, which is entirely realistic, that expenditure is not totally elastic. The so-called 'guns versus butter' thesis is a perennial in the military expenditure literature. In this instance we wish to examine to what extent military expenditure may be made at the expense of health and education expenditure.

The principal variables we use, all of which are expressed in both gross and relative form, are: total budgetary expenditure, balance on the budget, interest payment on the public debt, size of public debt, size of health and education expenditure.[12]

Findings

Our first set of findings pertains to the hypothesized relationship between overall budget size and military expenditure. In common with a number of other studies we find very powerful simple correlations between budget size and military expenditure.[13] To some extent, however, we would expect strongly positive relations due quite simply to the substantial variation across countries both in the size of military expenditure and budget. Our interest lies, however, in testing not for a size but for a budget effect. We may control for a size effect by regressing military expenditure on both GDP and budget (expecting if there is a budget effect to find that budget predicts to military expenditure controlling for GDP) or by regressing relative military expenditure on relative budget. Generally speaking we find evidence of a substantial and significant budget effect.[14]

We would argue, however, that this relationship is potentially seriously misleading primarily because the dependent variable is not only contained within but also can constitute a large part of the independent variable. A ready way around this difficulty is simply to subtract military expenditure from the total budget, which we now call the unadjusted budget, to give us an adjusted budget. A much sounder test of a budget effect then is to examine whether adjusted budget, controlling again for GDP, predicts to military expenditure.[15]

We find now that our results change dramatically to yield much less strong and less consistent evidence of a budget effect.[16] Before examining the implications of this, we need to consider the nature of the interpretation we attach to the budget effect.

One possibility, which would make overall budget size of little interest to us, is that relative adjusted budget size is little more than a measure of level of development. Thus, it might be argued that smaller budgets simply reflect levels of development in that lower levels of development either restrict an ability to collect revenues or provide a smaller base from which revenues may be raised. If this were the case then budget size and levels of development would be collinear and any simple relationship between military expenditure and budget would not indicate a true budget effect but rather a development effect, of which budget was a reflection. Though this argument certainly sounds plausible, it does not seem likely to us. We know that Third World countries in aggregate maintain much larger budgets than the OECD countries did at analogous levels of development which is not reflective of a generalized inability to raise revenues. Furthermore, levels of development, as measured by per capita income, are most certainly not collinear with relatively budget size.[17]

While the previous difficulty focused on the possibility that any relationship between military expenditure expenditure and budget may be spurious, a second problem refers to the issue of the validity of the indicator of budget size. Certainly within the developed countries budget size has been taken to reflect to a pronounced degree the politico-economic orientation of the government with larger and smaller budgets being indicative respectively of differing propensities to social democratic or liberal lines of development. We can think of no pressing reason why a liberal–social democratic continuum should predict to military expenditure, in which event we would not of course expect to find any budget effect. Though the liberal–social democratic issue is certainly not irrelevant for Third World countries, we would argue that this debate exists much more at a rhetorical than a practical level and as such does not hold the same significance as in the developed countries. Furthermore, if we were wrong in this context we would not run the risk of producing a spurious relationship.[18]

We are inclined to the view that we do indeed see a budgetary effect, which is one that taps a propensity to governmental control. The rather generalized growth of Third World budgets and the high levels that they have reached, by comparative and historical standards, indicate to us evidence of a widespread propensity for Third World governments to develop the budget as a means of consolidation or control. Within this we see some propensity for those states more strongly committed to establishing central control and direction to devote greater resources to the military.

Nonetheless it has to be emphasized that this budgetary effect is rather slight. Furthermore, returning to our earlier findings on the unadjusted budget, it will be recalled, even after size is controlled, that the relationship of military expenditure to the unadjusted budget is substantially stronger than that of military expenditure to the adjusted budget. Consequently, though it is correct to assert that countries with larger budgets have larger military expenditures, we infer that countries have larger budgets because they have larger military expenditure rather than they have larger military expenditures because they have larger budgets.

Our second area of investigation pertains to budget financing. Though it would be erroneous to equate larger government debts or greater annual budget deficits with poor or unsound economic performance, it is realistic to assume, other things being equal, that these variables do present to some extent a profile of the financial constraints confronting governments. Our general working hypothesis is that larger deficits or debts do to some degree restrict government expenditure latitude and as such would predict to lower levels of military expenditure.

Before proceeding to the results from this hypothesis, we may note some descriptive details of Third World budget financing. As we see from Table 4.2,

Table 4.2: Means values of balance on the budget, government debt
and interest payment on the debt as percentages of GDP
for Third World countries, selected years 1950–82

Year	Balance on budget	Government debt	Interest payment on debt
1950	−0.3	16.9	0.6
(N)	(13)	(18)	(12)
1954	−1.2	15.2	0.6
(N)	(21)	(12)	(18)
1958	−2.6	15.8	0.6
(N)	(27)	(15)	(20)
1962	−2.2	21.8	0.7
(N)	(34)	(17)	(24)
1966	−1.7	21.8	0.9
(N)	(41)	(20)	(27)
1970	−2.9	26.8	1.1
(N)	(57)	(22)	(37)
1974	−2.6	27.7	1.1
(N)	(72)	(41)	(56)
1978	−4.7	41.0	1.6
(N)	(68)	(38)	(54)
1982	−6.4	40.0	2.7
(N)	(49)	(28)	(47)

Third World countries are predominantly engaged in deficit financing, a tendency which generally speaking is becoming more pronounced.[19] Furthermore the magnitude of deficits is, in aggregate, increasing. Concomitantly general governmental debt is also increasing, with the foreign share of this debt also growing, so that servicing of this debt is becoming a larger component of budgetary expenditure.[20]

Our working hypothesis in the context of the balance on the budget would lead us to expect a positive relationship to military expenditure. Controlling for GDP, we do not find, however, any significant results.[21] It could be plausibly argued that we may be looking for the wrong form of relationship in that there may not be a uniform effect on military expenditure across surplus and deficit positions. It is possible, for instance, that a deficit may well constrain but a surplus may not stimulate military expenditure, in which event we would be in error in looking for a simple linear relationship. Adjusting our regression model to take account of this possibility, we still fail to produce any significant results.[22]

While budget balance is in our view a sound and valid indicator of financial constraints, it does, at least on an isolated annual basis, provide only a short-term measure of constraint. Any budget that is, for instance, in deficit in one year could have been in surplus in the preceding year. In this respect, budget balance does not then provide a measure of accumulated financial constraint and it is quite conceivable that a financial constraint effect may be present but in the guise of a more accumulated or longer-term than a shorter-term effect. To tap this possibility we consider the influence of the variables of government debt and interest payments on the debt.

These two variables, expectedly, are strongly correlated as in effect debt is a stock measure for which interest payment is a flow. Generally speaking, each of these variables, and debt in particular, predicts significantly and positively, even after GDP is controlled, to budget size. Furthermore each predicts significantly and negatively to surplus on the balance of the budget. Against a general trend of deficit financing, there seems to be something of a tendency for some governments to become locked into a vicious spiral, whereby larger debts lead to larger budgets to larger deficits to larger debts.

Turning specifically to an examination of the influence of our longer-term measures of financial constraints on military expenditure, we would expect, other things being equal, that relative government debt and relative interest payments would predict inversely to lower levels of relative military expenditure. Table 4.3 provides a survey of these and related results for one illustrative, though typical, test year. We can find no corroboration for our hypothesis.[23]

Table 4.3: Correlation matrix for relative military expenditure, relative unadjusted budget, relative adjusted budget, relative balance on budget, relative government debt, relative interest payments on debt, 1978

	Military expenditure	Unadjusted budget	Adjusted budget	Balance on budget	Government debt
Unadjusted budget	0.54[a]	—	—	—	—
Adjusted budget	0.31[a]	0.96[a]	—	—	—
Balance on budget	−0.04	−0.37[a]	−0.41[a]	—	—
Government debt	0.31	0.72[a]	0.72[a]	−0.54[a]	—
Interest payments on debt	0.14	0.48[a]	0.48[a]	−0.64[a]	0.88[a]

[a] Significance at 0.05 level or beyond.

In sum, we can find no evidence that military expenditure is responsive to government financial constraints of a short- or long-term variety. In this respect, then, we infer that military expenditure has a life largely independent of central financial constraints, indicative therefore on its part of a substantial degree of autonomy.

Our third and final area of budgetary investigation concerns expenditure on education and health. These two sectors entail infrastructure expenditures, generally held to be crucial both for development and the so-called physical quality of life, which are commonly presented as rivals to military expenditure. Our primary interest centres on using data from the behaviour of education and health expenditures as a vehicle for amplifying our understanding of military expenditure.

The first of three main conclusions we draw from this investigation is that while a substantial commitment is made by Third World countries to the growth and expansion of education and health expenditure, that commitment is not as high as in the area of military expenditure. In this respect military expenditure, then, is generally taken to be a higher priority.

The question of priority may be confronted in two ways. The more simple is to compare the relative proportions of GDP committed to the expenditures on the military, education and health. If Table 4.4 is compared with Table 2.2, we may see that generally greater resources are committed to the military than to either education or health.

Table 4.4: Relative education and health expenditure for Third World countries selected years 1950–80

	1950	1955	1960	1965	1970	1975	1980
Education expenditure							
Mean	1.01	1.33	2.08	2.76	3.08	3.07	3.58
Standard deviation	0.63	0.75	1.01	1.13	1.18	1.66	1.91
Health expenditure							
Mean	0.58	0.55	0.81	1.07	1.20	1.25	1.40
Standard deviation	0.42	0.28	0.41	0.48	0.54	0.79	0.90
(N)	(12)	(20)	(27)	(38)	(49)	(59)	(49)

A further and perhaps more telling insight into priority is to compare rates of growth of these different expenditures. Both education and health display significant positive rates of growth over time for an overwhelming majority of countries.[24] These rates of growth, furthermore, are generally higher for most countries than their rates of growth of GDP. They are, however, as indicated by paired t-tests, significantly lower than the rates of growth of military expenditure.[25]

Our second main conclusion, not dissimilar in general thrust to an argument that has been made above in the context of financial constraints, is that military expenditure seems to display greater independence or autonomy of movement than either education or health. We document this in two ways.

First, there are as we have already noted some striking similarities in these three areas of public expenditure. Each is generally increasing over time, usually at a rate of growth higher than GDP, across a majority of Third World countries. Despite a rather substantial and generalized expansion, there is of course variation in the commitment to each of these areas across Third World countries. The critical point, however, which may be seen in Table 4.5, is that variation in the commitment to military expenditure is substantially greater than to either education or health expenditure.[26] In other words, Third World countries as a whole move their education and health expenditures in a much narrower band than their military expenditure. This greater variability or volatility of military expenditure indicates to us then a greater independence or autonomy of movement.

Table 4.5: Coefficients of variability for relative military, education and health expenditure for Third World countries, selected years 1950–80

	1950	1955	1960	1965	1970	1975	1980
Military expenditure	0.77	0.77	1.07	1.06	1.18	1.36	1.08
Education expenditure	0.62	0.56	0.49	0.41	0.38	0.54	0.53
Health expenditure	0.72	0.51	0.51	0.44	0.45	0.63	0.64

A second illustration of this point concerns the comparative behaviour of military expenditure within countries.[27] Amalgamating education and health expenditure, we find that generally education–health expenditure moves in greater harmony than military expenditure with overall budgetary expansion.[28] The greater harmony or synchronization between budget size and education–health expenditure cannot be explained in terms of the size of education–health as opposed to military expenditure.[29] Rather we are inclined to the argument that the lower level of synchronization of military expenditure with budget is a reflection again of the greater independence of military expenditure. Third World governments are more inclined to move education and health expenditures in line with overall budget expansions and contractions. This leads us to infer that education–health expenditure is a rather more staple component of general government expenditure than military expenditure, which though of course ultimately entirely constrained by budget expenditure does show greater freedom or latitude in its movement.

Although military expenditure does seem to attract some special priority and enjoy a greater degree of autonomy, our third conclusion suggests that military expenditure is not detrimental to either education or health expenditure.

It might seem that there should be a zero-sum relationship between military and education or health spending in that a dollar spent on one cannot be spent on the other. In this event we would expect to find inverse relationships between relative military expenditure and relative education or health spending. This is not the case.[30] Furthermore, there are no signs of any inverse relationships between rates of growth of military expenditure and those of education or health.

Countries expanding their military expenditure more rapidly are not prone to lower rates of growth of education or health.[31]

The failure to find any significant inverse relations reflects a weakness in the opportunity cost type of reasoning posited in the zero-sum relationship. The zero-sum effect would hold only if the budget were held constant. In practice what happens, as we have already seen, is that countries with larger military expenditures also have larger budgets. Consequently, states with greater commitments to the military in effect can maintain their education and health commitments by expanding the budget, thereby obviating any necessity for military expenditure on the part of the government to be made at the expense of its education or health spending.

Summary

Approaching military expenditure from the perspective of the budget is not very productive as far as determinants of military expenditure are concerned. This approach does however contribute usefully both to a general understanding of military expenditure and some of its implications.

The only determinant influence we can isolate is manifested in what we have called the budget effect. The particular interpretation we favour is that countries more disposed to establish and consolidate central government control produce larger budgets and as an integral part of this drive commit themselves to larger military expenditures. This effect is, however, not only rather slight but also not consistent over time.

The rather more striking results pertain not to determinants but to the nature and implications of military expenditure. Thus, it is not so much that larger budgets drive larger military spending but that the latter results in the former. It seems rather that governments adopt a given level of military commitment largely independent of the budget and then simply expand the budget as necessary to incorporate this level of commitment. Somewhat in keeping with this, countries do not seem to be restrained by central government financial constraints, in which respect military expenditure appears to enjoy a substantial degree of autonomy. Evidently if countries wish to commit themselves to higher levels of military expenditure they will not be held back by central government financial difficulties. This picture seems to be further confirmed when military expenditure is compared and contrasted with the other and rather different expenditure areas of education and health. The evidence here underscores again a marked degree of autonomy on the part of military expenditure and points to a special preference or priority generally being attached to military expenditure. Precisely because countries seem to adjust their budgets to accommodate whatever level of military expenditure, this form of expenditure does not seem to take place to the detriment of education or health spending.

The budgetary analysis seems to point to the military as an area of expenditure that seems to enjoy some substantial independence or autonomy and which is accommodated by rather than accommodates to the budget.

Notes

1. This area above all others has been dominated by economists where there has been and continues to be a major dispute between Keynesians and monetarists over the relative importance of fiscal versus monetary management. Furthermore, even within that group who are strongly committed to the relative importance of fiscal management, there is dispute as to how extensively a government should commit itself to either a surplus or deficit as a way of managing demand. Political scientists have tended to focus on a narrower debate centring on the implications of a fiscal crisis. See e.g. J. O'Connor, *The Fiscal Crisis of the State* (New York: St Martin's Press, 1973); R. Rose and B.G. Peter, *Can Governments Go Bankrupt?* (London: Macmillan, 1979).

2. That state control has been increasing and that budget expansion is a key though not sole component of this we take to be largely uncontentious. Controversy rather has centred on what has driven the expansion and the implications of the expansion. Some argue that increasing state control is a function of economic and technological imperatives resulting in convergence; others see state control as more variable, being a function of the relative predominance of left and right forces; more left-wing writers see state control as a response to the contradictions in capitalism resulting in a temporary postponement of the collapse of capitalism. For some good illustrations of these very divergent views, see F. Castles, *The Social Democratic Image of Society* (London: Routledge & Kegan Paul, 1978); G. Esping Andersen, *Politics Against Markets* (Princeton: Princeton University Press, 1985); J.K. Galbraith, *The New Industrial State* (London: Hamish Hamilton, 1967); B. Jessop, *The Capitalist State* (Oxford: Martin Robertson, 1982); F.L. Pryor, *Public Expenditures on Communist and Capitalist Countries* (Homewood: Irwin, 1968); R. Rose (ed.), *Challenge to Governance* (London: Sage, 1980); R. Rose, *Understanding Big Government*, (London: Sage, 1984); A. Wilensky, *The Welfare State and Equality* (Berkeley: University of California Press, 1975).

3. The three aspects on which we have focused, fiscal management, political control and political choice, are not held to be autonomous or discrete but rather mutually overlapping. For instance, while we take the growth of the overall budget size to indicate an extension of generalized state control, the particular areas in which governments raise revenue or expend, what we have called political choice, also tell us something more about control. Thus, by virtue of expressing differential preferences across different sectors, the government can positively or negatively discriminate in favour of or against particular groups. The government can, in other words, attempt to influence or control particular sections of the populace by using the budget to bestow differential rewards and costs.

4. See e.g. P.T. Bauer, *Dissent on Development* (London: Weidenfeld & Nicolson, 1971); P.T. Bauer, *Equality, the Third World and Economic Delusion* (London: Weidenfeld & Nicolson, 1981); H.G. Johnson, 'A Word to the Third World', *Encounter*, Oct. 1971.

5. M.B. Krauss, *Development Without Aid* (New York: McGraw Hill, 1983).

6. Independent Commission on International Development Issues, *North–South (Cambridge: MIT Press, 1980); J. Tinbergen et al., Reshaping the International Order* (New York: Dutton, 1976).

7. See e.g. M.Ul Haq, *The Poverty Curtain* (New York: Columbia University Press, 1976); P. Streeten, *First Things First* (Oxford: Oxford University Press, 1981).

8. We regress relative budget size over time for each country. If we find a significant equation with a positive b coefficient, then that coefficient represents a significant estimate of an annual increment or linear growth rate of the budget.

9. Coefficients of variation indicate that the generalized growth in Third World relative budget size is more homogeneous than that of relative military expenditure.

10. Mean relative budget sizes for the OECD countries for matching years to Table 4.1 are: 17.2 (1950), 17.3 (1954), 20.7 (1958), 19.8 (1962), 21.7 (1966), 23.2 (1970), 25.2 (1974), 32.4 (1978), 36.7 (1982). By the mid-1970s Third World countries had achieved a level of relative budgetary expenditure that would have appeared high to the OECD countries in 1950.

11. For instance, by 1978 Third World states had achieved a relative budget level slightly in excess of the OECD countries' level of 1970, while having in 1978 a mean per capita income just under a quarter of that of the OECD countries in 1970.

12. Our preferred source for these figures is the annual publication of the International Monetary Fund titled *Government Financial Statistics* (IMF GFS). This gives figures of a generally standardized and comparable form from the early 1970s. Before that date the IMF *Financial Statistics* has been used as long as a substantial matching overlap was found. Only in exceptional circumstances was the UN *Statistical Yearbook* used. The budget figures pertain to central government and include both current and capital accounts. Surplus or deficit refers to balance on revenue and expenditure. Government debt relates only to direct debt of the central government and excludes loans guaranteed by the government. Where figures are given in fiscal years, we have made simple proportionate adjustments to calendar years.

13. The simple correlations between gross military expenditure and total gross budgetary expenditure for each of our test years are: 0.90 (1982), 0.90 (1978), 0.91 (1974), 0.92 (1970), 0.89 (1966), 0.90 (1962), 0.81 (1958), 0.77 (1954).

14. Stepwise regressions of absolute military expenditure on both GDP and total government expenditure indicate that government expenditure is a better predictor than GDP in five of eight test years (in fact all test years except 1954, 1958 and 1966). This would still leave us with a size effect which we can most easily remove by regressing relative military expenditure on relative budget. These yield significant correlations in all years except 1954 and 1958 of: 0.39 (1982), 0.54 (1978), 0.60 (1974), 0.54 (1970), 0.30 (1966), 0.54 (1962).

15. If, for example, all countries committed exactly the same proportion of their GDP to the adjusted budget, then we would find no relationship between relative military expenditure and relative adjusted budget. Were we now to add in relative military expenditure to the adjusted budget, giving us the unadjusted budget, we would find a perfect relationship between relative military expenditure and relative unadjusted budget. We would therefore be finding a perfect relationship between military expenditure and budget, which, in terms of budget size explaining military expenditure, would be quite invalid.

16. In stepwise regressions of military expenditure on GDP and adjusted budget, the latter appears as a significant predictor in only two test years (1974, 1978). The simple correlations between relative military expenditure and relative adjusted budget reduce substantially across all years as compared with the correlations between relative military expenditure and relative unadjusted budget. In fact, the correlations are significant now in only three test years: 0.31 (1978), 0.38 (1974), 0.27 (1970).

17. There are in fact positive correlations between budget size and per capita income but they are very weak.

18. If for instance the liberal–social democratic positions were very marked in the Third World countries and did predict to budget size, then, assuming there was no relationship between liberal–social democratic position and military expenditure, budget

would not predict to military expenditure. We are not then in danger of isolating a confounded result.

19. The percentage of cases running deficits are: 71 (1954), 66 (1958), 82 (1962), 83 (1966), 86 (1970), 81 (1974), 79 (1978), 90 (1982).
20. The percentage shares of foreign debt in total government debt are: 14 (1950), 17 (1954), 19 (1958), 29 (1962), 37 (1966), 38 (1970), 48 (1974), 48 (1978), 61 (1982).
21. The variable of balance on the budget has both negative and positive signs. We cannot of course take logarithms of negative values. Consequently we take the log of an absolute value and then reinsert the sign. In only one test year (1962) are we able to find balance on the budget appearing as a significant estimator of military expenditure once GDP is controlled. (The beta coefficients for GDP and balance are respectively 0.98 and 0.19, indicating the former is considerably more important.)
22. Instead of regressing relative military expenditure on relative budget balance, we regress our dependent variable on the relative absolute balance, a dummy for the sign of the balance, and an interaction term for the dummy and absolute balance. This three-variables model then permits us to test for different slopes for both deficit and surplus sides of the balance.
23. As will be noticed from Table 4.1 there is a serious lack of data both on interest payments and especially on debt. This accounts, for instance, in Table 4.3 for the simple correlations between relative military expenditure on the one hand and adjusted budget and debt on the other being significant in the former but not in the latter case (which has fewer degrees of freedom). We have checked that military expenditure does not vary in mean size across these cases with and without debt figures. Thus, while we would of course much prefer more comprehensive debt figures, we do not consider any systematic distortion is taking place. In none of our test years do debt or interest payment predict significantly as we would hypothesize. In fact in two test years there are significant associations in the wrong direction.
24. Logged regressions of education and health over time for each country produce significant positive equation in 91 and 88 per cent of cases. This growth furthermore is very stable – mean R^2 values for these regressions produce scores of 85 and 81 respectively for education and health.
25. The mean rates of growth for military, education and health expenditure, which are extracted from regressions of each of these logged expenditures over time for each country, are respectively 7.96, 5.99 and 4.81. We have more cases where data is available for military expenditure than for the other two variables. If we compute military expenditure rates of growth for only those cases on which we have education and health data, the rate of growth changes negligibly for military expenditure from a global mean of 7.96 to the smaller population mean of 8.11. The higher rates of growth for military expenditure are not however found for every single case. In fact education and health growth rates are higher than military expenditure in 30 and 23 per cent of cases respectively. Nonetheless, paired t-tests show military expenditure rates of growth to be higher than either education or health rates of growth at a significance level beyond 0.01.
26. Other things being equal we would expect variation to increase with mean. The coefficient of variability controls for this by dividing variation by mean value.
27. Table 4.5 reports data across countries. It is conceivable that this could lead to wrong inferences on volatility, for which we can correct by checking the argument by looking at behaviour within countries over time.

28. We amalgamate health and education expenditure due to the relatively small size of the former. We find significant correlations between education–health and budget size in 82 per cent of cases compared with 58 per cent of cases for military expenditure. Furthermore, education–health is a better predictor of budget size than military expenditure in 71 per cent of cases.

29. Some education–health expenditure is much the same as that of military expenditure, it could not be argued that the one fits budget more closely due to a greater weight in the budget.

30. The correlations between relative military expenditure on the one hand and relative education or health spending on the other for each of our eight main test years yield either insignificant or significant small positive values but never significant negative ones.

31. In fact if anything the obverse is true. Taking each country's rate of growth of military, education, and health spending, we find the military and education rates of growth correlate at a small but significantly positive value of 0.34, while those of military and health correlate at 0.44.

5 Military Expenditure and International Interactions

Introduction

We have thus far mainly focused on potential determinants of military expenditure which are primarily domestic in origin. This is the first of three chapters where the emphasis switches explicitly to the international arena. The basic rationale for this chapter stems from two rival sets of prescriptions to be found in the so-called realist and idealist schools.[1]

To realist writers the basic building block of the international system is the state. The principal objective of state behaviour has been taken to be the preservation of state independence or autonomy. Such a preoccupation, however, has never been held to imply autarchy but on the contrary has presupposed some degree of state interaction. The pursuit of independence within a 'system of states' has generally been held by realists to produce a condition of chronic insecurity. To avoid this danger it is incumbent on states, according to realist prescriptions, to develop an 'international society of states', which is essentially a set of common values, institutions and organizations capable of moderating state interaction.[2]

This scenario has been adamantly criticized by idealist writers for whom the pursuit of national interest in an anarchic international system has been a constant source of insecurity and the underlying cause of interstate war. To obviate this problem the idealist prescription is that it is necessary to foster international integration, by which is understood the progressive transfer of state autonomy and sovereignty to supranational bodies. A principal vehicle for promoting international integration, which as a process would result in the condition of supranationalism, is seen to be the enhancement of international interaction. Increasing interaction, enjoying the status of a necessary though insufficient condition, would foster integration by dint of eroding the salience of national boundaries.[3]

Moving from the more prescriptive to the more empirical level, the postwar period has undoubtedly seen an interesting tension or dynamic between the forces encouraging on the one hand a progression toward integration and on the other the enhancement of the state. Pointing to such developments as the growth of international organizations, of international banks, of multinational corporations, of the blurring of domestic and foreign policy, of the expansion of the international trade and monetary systems, of the qualitative changes of the communications revolution, of the development of problem areas especially in the ecological and resource areas that do not respect national boundaries, some writers have inferred a strong process toward international integration. While some regard this process as having introduced a qualitatively new era of inter-dependence, others go further to suggest the emergence of a world society.[4]

Against this other writers point to the continued viability and adaptability of the state. They argue, for instance, that intergovernmental organizations are dominated by governments and controlled, expectedly, by the most powerful states; multinational corporations are not seen to have eroded state sovereignty; governments are held to have responded to changes in trade or monetary patterns by increasing their monitoring activities over these flows and incorporating them into national policy making; major formal moves towards integration, of which perhaps the European Community is perhaps the most impressive example, are seen to have stymied at least as far as the development of supranationalism is concerned; many ecological and resource issues are held to have been overstated particularly in their global impact and to have been accommodated by new regional intergovernmental organizations.[5] While such writers do not dispute the growth of international interaction, they do contest the direction in which this interaction is leading. Rather than eroding the state, increased interaction, it is argued, has enhanced the position of the state.

The Third World has not of course been immune to these two processes. The breakdown of colonial empires and the establishment of a substantial number of new states has been taken by realists in particular to indicate, though not without some qualifications, a major expansion and enhancement of the state system. Furthermore, Third World countries, through their governments, foreign offices and embassies, have developed many of the formal manifestations of sovereign states. They have moreover readily joined major international organizations, spawned their own international organizations, and through them have voiced many major policies, such as the demands for a New International Economic Order. All these developments are readily consonant with the realist perspective. Critical among these developments, all Third World countries, many of which were starting from scratch, have developed one of the most powerful defining attributes of a state, namely a national military. At the same time, Third World states could be said from the integration or interdependence perspective to have involved themselves both rapidly and extensively in the international system.

If we are correct in calling attention to the two important drives of integration and enhanced nation state development, it is in principle at least of some substantial interest to explore the relationship between Third World international inter-action, which we take to be a necessary though not sufficient condition of inte-gration, and military expenditure, which we take to be one of the major hallmarks of state sovereignty and thereby one of the major impediments to integration.

On the basis of this general line of reasoning, or rationale, we may now state our general working hypothesis. Other things being equal, we would anticipate that an idealist perspective would predict a negative relationship between inter-national interaction and military expenditure on the grounds that higher levels of international interaction would reduce the salience of the state and thereby of the military. We would anticipate in turn that a realist perspective would predict a null or positive relationship. We adopt as our general working hypothesis the null or positive relationship between levels of international interaction and military expenditure that we would associate with realist thinking.[6] Four more specific reasons constitute the rationale for or explanation of this selection.

First, the prediction from increased interaction to reduced nation-state salience would seem to us to imply that states either command no resources to resist and/or are willing to succumb to their transformation. Not only does it seem to us that neither of these conditions is valid but also that states traditionally have shown themselves to be actively opposed to their demise. One, again very traditional, mechanism that states may employ in order to preserve their identity, i.e. to resist transformation, is the maintenance and development of a national military.[7]

Second, we reason that increased interaction will foster integration only if states display a large degree of commonality of purpose. If, on the other hand, states manifest pronounced differences in substantive policies and goals, i.e. display competing and conflicting interests, then increased interaction far from stimulating integration may well work against it as states respond to increased awareness of differences in interests by reinforcing one of the primary instruments of autonomy, namely the military.

Third, even if the international system is characterized as a 'society' rather than a 'system of states', it would still seem to engender a substantial degree of ambiguity and uncertainty. Heightened international interaction, from which we infer heightened international sensitivity, would therefore increase, other things being equal, a sense of uncertainty to which again a consistent response could take the form of enhanced military expenditure.

Fourth, we postulate a diffusion or demonstration effect from high-income countries. As Third World states have become independent members of the international state system, they have not joined a system of equals. On the contrary, they have entered a hierarchical system, in which the rules and patterns of interaction are very unequally set by the high-income countries. Consequently we would expect a substantial degree of imitative behaviour, of varying degrees of spontaneity, whereby Third World countries respond to referrent norms set by the high-income countries. In the military sphere, Third World countries would see in the high-income countries military capabilities substantially greater than theirs. We reason that the higher the level of international interaction, the more powerful the demonstration or diffusion effect from the referrent norms and therefore the higher the level of imitative behaviour, which in our particular case would entail higher levels of military spending.

Ideally for our set of independent variables we would like to take a number of agreed operational indicators of the process of international integration. Despite a substantial literature on integration, such agreed operational indicators simply do not exist. Consequently we are obliged to focus on an array of interaction variables which we order initially by substantive area of interaction. Although our interest in these variables pertains to some degree to their substantive content, it also initially pertains to the capacity of these variables to operationalize the more theoretical content of heightened international awareness, and sensitivity and diffusion. The main clusters are: foreign direct investment and foreign production, trade, diplomatic ties, and arms imports. We examine these interactions not only in aggregate but also in major bloc groupings.

The first cluster comprises: investment income, which is the return on foreign direct investment and as such provides a stock measure; foreign direct investment, which provides a flow measure; and net factor income from abroad, which provides some measure, albeit not perfect unfortunately, of foreign penetration of an economy.[8] The second cluster, that of trade, comprises: volume of exports and imports, size of international liquidity holdings, and diversification of exports and imports by destination and origin.[9] The third cluster consists of number of embassies accredited by and to the country.[10] The final cluster is defined by arms imports.[11] The major bloc groupings we use are OECD, COMECON (Europe) and Third World, where within each of the first two clusters we disaggregate both the United States and the Soviet Union. Bloc interactions are examined in the area of trade, diplomatic ties and arms imports.

Findings

From our first cluster of interaction variables, that of foreign direct investment and production, we can find no real corroboration for our general working hypothesis.

Foreign direct investment together with economic aid, and more recently and more erratically commercial bank loans, represent the major means of capital transfers to the Third World. Not surprisingly perhaps, given this importance, foreign direct investment has figured prominently in controversies over development. At one extreme, market liberals see it as the primary vehicle for augmenting investment and thereby promoting development; at the other extreme, socialist writers have seen it as a means for diffusing capitalism, thereby distorting development.[12] While being diametrically opposed on the development impact of foreign direct investment, both extremes would concur that foreign direct investment, for better or worse, does represent a major means of international integration. While in bivariate terms both investment income and foreign direct investment are significantly and positively associated with military expenditure, once we control for country size we can find no evidence that either predicts positively to military expenditure. Indeed there is some evidence, though it is not strong, of the opposite effect.[13]

Net factor income provides a measure of the balance of a country's production overseas with foreign production in that country. For most Third World countries this balance is negative.[14] Other things being equal, our working hypothesis would predict that military expenditure would increase as both positive and negative balances increased. Though we see this relationship in bivariate terms, it does not appear once we control for GDP.[15] There are no indications, however, that higher positive or negative balances depress military expenditure.[16] The one sign of some minor corroboration of our hypothesis is that a positive balance does predict to military expenditure.[17] Though we are inclined to view any inference from this with some caution, a positive, as opposed to negative, balance would, other things being equal, indicate a relative predominance of the national economy over foreign controlled parts of the economy. In other words when the balance of interaction, in this case measured by national over foreign product, is in favour of and in this sense controlled by the Third World country, then there is a propensity for higher levels of military expenditure.[18]

In aggregate, though private direct economic involvement may well constitute one of the most important means of international economic interaction, we are obliged to conclude that we can find no real support for the hypothesis that it would predict to higher levels of military expenditure.

The second set of interaction variables focuses on trade. The first of two principal measures is export and import volume, which when expressed as a percentage of GDP represent the propensity of a country to trade. As this measure increases, and as concomitantly trade becomes more important to the economy of a country, we infer a greater degree of international involvement and heightened international sensitivity. The second of the two measures is export and import diversification. It is conceivable that a country could well maintain a high propensity to trade, but conduct this trade with, in the extreme, only one country. Though trade in this instance would be unquestionably important for the economy, it would nonetheless not entail a high level of international exposure. This low level of exposure would, however, be caught by trade diversification.

Table 5.1 contains some descriptive statistics, showing a generally high and increasing propensity to trade combined with a growing diversification of exports by commodity, of exports by origin and of imports by source.[19] Generally speaking, controlling for size, the propensity to trade is not quite as high as that of

Table 5.1: Mean values of propensity to trade and diversification measures, selected years 1954–82

	1954	1958	1962	1966	1970	1974	1978	1982
Exports as % GDP	15.9	16.0	15.6	18.2	19.7	26.6	21.8	20.1
Imports as % GDP	14.4	16.1	16.8	17.8	17.5	21.8	23.6	23.3
Diversification of exports by destination	50	47	47	44	42	40	40	35
Diversification of imports by origin	47	44	45	42	39	36	36	35
Diversification of exports by commodity	63	60	57	57	56	57	57	50

the OECD countries but it is certainly moving in that direction. Furthermore, only those Third World countries with the highest levels of diversification approximate to the OECD countries. We do nonetheless see clear movements to the OECD model, and in this respect a display not only of higher levels of interaction but also of imitative behaviour.

Generally speaking, we find some clear, though not overwhelming, corroboration for our general working hypothesis from our trade variables.

In bivariate terms gross exports and imports each show highly significant relations to gross military expenditure. The relationship which interests us, however, is not absolute trade but propensity to trade, for which we need to control for size in the form of GDP. Forcing GDP into a regression equation and then allowing the trade variables to enter in a stepwise manner enables us to achieve this. Such an exercise produces a significant propensity to trade effect in each of the last three test years. Rather more impressive results come from the diversification variables. Table 5.2 and 5.2(A), summarizing these results, show that trade diversification generally speaking has a more consistent and powerful effect.[20]

Though assuredly not overwhelming, the results in particular from trade

Table 5.2: Regression results of military expenditure on GDP and trade and on GDP, trade and diversification measures, selected years 1954–82

	Regressions of military expenditure on trade with forced entry of GDP	R^2	Regression of military expenditure on GDP, trade, and diversification	R^2
1954	0.97 (GDP) (0.87)	0.75	no change	
1958	0.97 (GDP) (0.84)	0.70	0.88 (GDP) − 0.01 (DIVED) (0.77) (−0.27)	0.77
1962	1.14 (GDP) (0.88)	0.78	0.93 (GDP) − 0.01 (DIVED) (0.72) (−0.29)	0.84
1966	0.99 (GDP) +0.22 (IL) (0.75) (0.19)	0.82	1.14 (GDP) − 0.01 (DIVMS) (0.87) (−0.76)	0.83
1970	1.15 (GDP) (0.87)	0.76	1.10 (GDP) − 0.02 (DIVMS) (0.84) (−0.19)	0.79
1974	0.69 (GDP) +0.46(E) (53) (0.37)	0.78	0.65 (GDP) + 0.48 (M) (0.50) (0.34) −0.02 (DIVMS) (−0.24)	0.83
1978	0.26 (GDP) +0.54 (M) (0.21) (0.43) + 0.29 (IL) (0.30)	0.82	0.67 (M) + 0.35 (IL) (0.53) (0.37) −0.01 (DIVED) (−0.15)	0.84
1982	0.29 (GDP) +0.48 (M) (0.24) (0.38) + 0.30 (IL) (0.32)	0.82	0.67 (M) + 0.37 (IL) (0.53) (0.40) −0.02 (DIVMS) (−0.17)	0.84

Table 5.2(A): Regression results of relative military expenditure on propensity to trade and diversification measures selected years 1954–82

	Equations	R^2
1954	NS	—
1958	−0.01 (DIVED) (−0.52)	0.27
1962	−0.01 (DIVED) (−0.58)	0.33
1966	−0.01 (DIVED) (−0.40)	0.16
1970	−0.02 (DIVMS) (−0.45)	0.20
1974	−0.02 (DIVED) (−0.52)	0.27
1978	0.54 (PE) −0.02 (DIVED) (0.39) (−0.39)	0.31
1982	0.51 (PE) −0.02 (DIVED) (0.41) (−0.42)	0.32

diversification are encouraging and would lead us to expect further support from our third cluster of variables, that of diplomatic ties. Interestingly diplomatic associations are more closely related to trade diversification, as we see in Table 5.3, than either is to propensity to trade. While trade diversification is undoubtedly a measure based on an explicitly economic variable, it does seem to us in its implications to have a markedly less direct economic content than propensity to trade. In this respect it is not perhaps surprising that while trade diversification is far from collinear with diplomatic ties, a more explicitly political variable, each of these two are more closely related than to propensity to trade.[21]

Table 5.3: Correlation matrix of number of embassies, trade diversification and propensity to trade, 1978

	EMBTOT	EMTTOT	DIVED	DIVMS	PE
EMTTOT	0.86*	—	—	—	—
DIVED	−0.30*	−0.26*	—	—	—
DIVMS	−0.39*	−0.29*	0.44*	—	—
PE	−0.06	−0.15	0.13	−0.04	—
PM	−0.17	−0.21	0.09	−0.23	0.63*

*Significant at 0.05 level or beyond.

Again we would emphasize that we are not positing that diplomatic ties themselves directly drive military expenditure. Rather we take diplomatic ties to be an operational indicator of international awareness or sensitivity and it is that process that we hypothesize underlies higher levels of military expenditure. Once more we see in purely descriptive terms, from Table 5.4, a generally impressive and sustained growth in Third World international interactions, as measured by the mean number of embassies accredited by and to Third World countries.[22]

Table 5.4: Mean number of embassies accredited by and to Third World Countries, selected years 1954–82

	1954	1958	1962	1966	1970	1974	1978	1982
Mean number embassies accredited by	22	25	23	26	30	33	38	40
Mean number embassies accredited to	27	25	22	23	27	31	35	37

The clearest support for our general hypothesis comes from the correlations between relative military expenditure and number of embassies, where we find a significant positive association in half of our test years.[23] Indeed we would be surprised if these results were not more powerful had we a more sensitive indicator of diplomatic associations.[24] Introducing diplomatic ties into regression equations containing the trade variables, we find that diplomatic ties are not as powerful a predictor as trade diversification but nonetheless on a number of occasions coherently expand our equations.[25]

Our third cluster of variables focuses on arms imports, in which context we again hypothesize a positive relationship from arms imports to military expenditure. The relationship, as we express it, does seem to us to be somewhat contentious. Consequently before examining our results we confront what we take to be the principal likely objections.

First, it might be argued that a positive relation between arms imports and military expenditure is tautologous on the grounds that since arms imports must be included in overall military expenditure, then higher levels of the former must be associated with higher levels of the latter.

Second, it might be argued that the relationship between arms imports and military expenditure is an artifact. Though we can think of no convincing argument as to why military expenditure would independently explain arms imports, it seems eminently plausible to us that arms imports could simply be a reflection of military expenditure, and thereby the relationship would be an artifact. Imagine, for instance, beyond a certain constant level that military expenditure levels were predicted by the occurrence of, say, interstate war. As states responded to war by increasing their levels of military expenditure, it could be that the form they chose so to do would be through higher levels of arms imports. In this event arms imports, though of course positively correlated with military expenditure, would not explain military expenditure. Both in fact would in effect be a function of war. Consequently arms imports far from explaining military expenditure would simply describe how military expenditure would expand as both these variables responded to war. The relationship between arms imports and military expenditure would then be an artifact.

Against these two arguments, we would argue, first, that the relationship of arms imports to military expenditure could only be a tautology if it were the case that the relationship could take only one form. The relationship could, however, take a variety of different forms. If countries simply switched part of their weapons budget from domestic to international procurement, then, controlling for size, there would be no relationship between arms imports and military expenditure. This would hold furthermore irrespective of the proportion that was switched as long as the proportions were randomly distributed across GDP levels. Or, there could, again controlling for size of country through a variable like GDP, be an inverse relationship. This could happen in either of two circumstances. First, the importing country may follow the strategy of import substitution and buy arms on the international market which would be cheaper than the equivalent that it could produce domestically. Second, the imported arms could be sufficiently qualitatively superior that they could replace a larger volume of expenditure either on domestically procured weapons or manpower. Since the relationship of arms imports to military expenditure is then variable it cannot conceivably be tautologous.

The artifact argument is decidedly more problematic and most certainly cannot be dismissed in the categoric manner of the tautology charge. Nonetheless, if arms imports were a function of a variable, such as war, which also simultaneously explained military expenditure, then arms imports would be collinear with that variable or variables. Our regression equations, however, would pick up this problem, as we would find that arms imports had a low tolerance value, i.e. a large part of the variance of arms imports would be explained by other independent variables in the regression equation. Our main difficulty lies, of course, with variables that we may have overlooked. Thus, while we can be sure that the arms import–military expenditure relationship is not an artifact produced by any of the variables contained in this study, we cannot entirely dismiss the artifact charge as we may have overlooked critical determinants of military expenditure.

Against this background but more particularly because we posit a more direct relationship to military expenditure from arms imports than in the case of the other interaction variables we have examined thus far, it is incumbent on us to specify rather more precisely how arms imports may influence military expenditure.

If there is indeed a positive relation between arms imports and military expenditure, controlling for size through GDP, then countries importing higher volumes of arms are spending more in the military than would be expected from their size alone. The higher volume of arms import cannot reflect either import substitution (otherwise arms imports would be a negative estimator) or simple switching (otherwise arms imports would have no relationship to military expenditure). Rather it must reflect a stimulative effect, which we suggest is produced through two principal mechanisms.

The first of these is what we might call an available demonstration effect. Third World countries looking to the high-income ones would see highly developed military systems, which we take, following a fairly conventional line, to be strongly supported though far from totally determined by a substantial military–industrial complex.[26] Both domestic pressure from these countries, much of it originating within the military-industrial complex, and competition between these countries have in effect made available to Third World countries almost any conventional weapon system short of the very latest models. If they so choose, Third World countries, in the military sector, can approximate to a high-income country.

The second mechanism pertains to a proliferation effect, both horizontal and vertical, within the weapons systems themselves. Modern weapons systems, by dint of being so highly complex, are highly interdependent. As such one weapon demands another and so on in a process of horizontal proliferation. Modern weapons systems are also subject to a rapid rate of innovation, and hence obsolescence, and as such manifest vertical proliferation. This proliferation or escalatory or action–reaction form of development, which we take to be well documented, is sustained again by a military–industrial complex.[27]

These two mechanisms, the available demonstration and proliferation effects, constitute what we may call an imported military–industrial complex effect, for which we see arms imports as the conduit. We are led therefore to posit that the greater the volume of arms imports, the stronger the imported military–industrial complex effect, and consequently the stronger the stimulative effect on military expenditure.

Turning to consider our findings, we may note first some descriptive statistics on the behaviour of arms imports. Arms imports have increased over time, which is not *per se* terribly surprising.[28] In order to gain some idea of the significance of this increase, we need to place it in some comparative perspective. The simplest way to do this is to express arms imports as a percentage of GDP, so that if this ratio increases over time we are witnessing a more rapid rate of growth of arms imports than GDP. Unfortunately the accounting system for measuring arms imports does not permit this. Nonetheless since we have measures in constant terms, it does make sense to examine growth within each variable and by comparing these rates we can achieve much the same result. Table 5.5 looks at such growth rates for the variables of arms imports, GDP and per capita income. From this table we see that GDP has expanded more rapidly than per capita income (due to faster population than GDP growth) and that arms imports in turn have expanded more rapidly than GDP.

Moving beyond the descriptive findings our results show a generally strong

Table 5.5: Proportionate increases in arms imports, GDP and per capita GDP, from selected years to 1978 and 1982

	To 1978			To 1982		
	Arms imports	GDP	GDP p.c.	Arms imports	GDP	GDP p.c.
1954	6.4	2.6	2.0	7.6	3.3	2.1
1958	3.8	2.1	2.0	4.5	2.8	2.1
1962	5.4	2.4	1.5	6.4	3.1	1.5
1966	4.7	2.3	1.5	5.5	3.0	1.6
1970	2.3	1.9	1.4	2.8	2.5	1.5
1974	1.7	1.3	1.0	2.0	1.7	1.0
1978	—	—	—	1.2	1.3	1.0

positive relationship of arms imports to military expenditure. These results may be presented through several cumulative stages.

In the first stage we profile arms imports as a dummy variable, measuring arms imports in other words simply in terms of their presence or absence.[29] Regressions of gross military expenditure on GDP and the dummy and of relative military expenditure on the dummy alone show a consistent and positive influence of arms imports on military expenditure.[30] In other words irrespective of a country's size, arms imports substantially increase military expenditure – in fact arms imports, admittedly controlling only for GDP, roughly double both absolute and relative military expenditure.[31]

A more stringent test, our second stage, is to introduce the dummy into equations containing not only GDP but also the leading interaction variables we have found to be significant estimators.[32] The results are no longer as impressive, though this is likely to be due to the rather simplistic form in which we have thus far measured arms imports.[33]

At a third stage we categorize arms imports in terms of zero, small, medium and large volume.[34] Substituting these variables into the above equation in place of the dummy, we find significant equations across all years, bar relative military expenditure in 1954.[35] These results, summarized in Tables 5.6 and 5.6(A) which may be compared with these of 5.2 and 5.2(A), interestingly show differential impacts across the varying levels of arms imports. Generally, low arms importers as far as absolute and relative military expenditure are concerned cannot be told apart from these countries that do not import arms. Medium-level importers generally, though not always, will have higher levels of either form of military expenditure, whereas high importers always have higher levels of military expenditure.[36]

In sum, there is some impressive evidence for a strong relationship of arms imports to military expenditure. We see in general no sign of any import substitution or replacement effects. There are signs of switching though this is confined

Table 5.6: Regression results of military expenditure on GDP, trade, trade diversification and levels of arms imports, selected years 1958–82

Year	Equation				R^2
1958:	−0.11 (AI1) + (NS)	0.25 (AI2) + (NS)	0.46 (AI3) + (0.28)	0.77 (GDP) (0.67)	0.80
1962:	0.32 (AI1) + (0.21) −0.01 (DIVMS) + (−0.19)	0.63 (AI2) + (0.36) 0.27 (IL) (0.24)	0.69 AI3) + (0.31)	0.49 (GDP) (0.38)	0.89
1966:	0.06 (AI1) + (NS) −0.01 (DIVMS) + (−0.11)	0.31 (AI2) + (0.20) 0.21(IL) (0.18)	0.59 (AI3) + (0.26)	0.73 (GDP) (0.56)	0.88
1970:	0.04 (AI1) + (NS) −0.01 (DIVMS) (−0.11)	0.28 (AI2) + (0.16)	0.62 (AI3) + (0.32)	0.88 (GDP) (0.66)	0.85
1974:	−0.02 (AI1) + (NS) −0.02 (DIVMS) + (−0.18)	0.22 (AI2) + (NS) 0.28(E) (0.23)	0.52 (AI3) + (0.29)	0.56 (GDP) (0.43)	0.86
1978:	0.19 (AI1) + (NS) +0.42 (M) − (0.33)	0.37 (AI2) + (0.21) 0.01 (DIVED) (−0.11)	0.65 (AI3) + (0.40)	0.33 (IL) (0.35)	0.88
1982:	−0.01 (AI1) + (NS) −0.02 (DIVMS) + (−0.16)	0.16 (AI2) + (NS) 0.34 (IL) (0.37)	0.44 (AI3) + (0.27)	0.50 (GDP) (0.41)	0.88

primarily to low levels of arms imports and to a much lesser extent to medium levels. More commonly medium levels and especially high levels appear to have a stimulative effect on military expenditure. We conclude therefore, following our earlier reasoning, that an imported military industrial complex, as transmitted through arms imports, does indeed contribute to an explanation of higher levels of military expenditure.

Our final area of investigation on the subject of international interactions focuses on an attempt to ascertain whether Third World military expenditure varies systematically in terms of Third World countries' differential interaction across different blocs of countries. We examine the interactions of diplomatic ties, trade and arms imports across blocs defined by the OECD countries (separating out additionally the USA), the COMECON (Europe) countries (separating out the USSR), and the Third World. Frankly, for reasons that will shortly become clear, this investigation proves fruitless. It does however produce

Table 5.6A: Regression results of relative military expenditure on per capita GDP, trade, propensity to trade, trade diversification and levels of arms imports, selected years 1958–82

Year	Equation				R^2
1958:	0.31 (AI1) + (0.46)	0.52 (AI2) + (0.78)	0.73 (AI3) – (0.82)	0.39 (E) (–0.58)	0.64
	–0.01 (DIVED) (–0.33)				
1962:	0.20 (AI1) + (NS)	0.39 (AI2) + (0.46)	0.46 (AI3) – (0.42)	0.28 (E) (–0.51)	0.56
	–0.01 (DIVED) (–0.63)				
1966:	–0.01 (AI1) + (NS)	0.22 (AI2) + (0.30)	0.46 (AI3) + (0.43)	0.26 (PIL) (0.24)	0.40
	–0.01 (DIVMS) (–0.22)				
1970:	0.10 (AI1) + (NS)	0.27 (AI2) + (0.29)	0.53 (AI3) – (0.53)	0.01 (DIVMS) (–0.27)	0.41
1974:	0.00 (AI1) + (NS)	0.17 (AI2) + (NS)	0.43 (AI3) – (0.46)	0.02 (DIVMS) (–0.46)	0.48
	–0.56 (GDP) + (–0.85)	0.48 (M) (0.67)			
1978:	0.26 (AI1) + (0.26)	0.32 (AI2) + (0.35)	0.62 (AI3) – (0.72)	0.30 (GDPPC) (–0.33)	0.53
	+0.64 (PE) – (0.47)	0.01 (DIVMS) (–0.27)			
1982:	0.08 (AI1) + (NS)	0.12 (AI2) + (NS)	0.36 (AI3) – (0.45)	0.02 (DIVMS) (–0.37)	0.45
	+ 0.44 (PE) (0.36)				

a number of descriptive results, which though somewhat tangential to our major concern, are actually of some interest. As a form of descriptive footnote to this chapter, we profile briefly some of these results.

As we see from Table 5.7, Third World diplomatic ties are expanding. Consistently, Third World countries extend a greater proportion of their embassies to each other than any other bloc. This proportion is furthermore increasing over time predominantly at the expense of the OECD countries. However, if we take account of the number of countries in which embassies could be established, in effect providing then a measure of relative priority, the COMECON group by the 1980s has about the right number, the Third World is rather under-represented, while the OECD countries have roughly twice as many embassies accredited to them from the Third World as they should. Thus, while in absolute terms Third World countries favour each other, in relative

Table 5.7: Mean percentages of Third World embassies accredited to the OECD, COMECON and the Third World, selected years 1954–82

Year	Embassies accredited to			
	OECD	COMECON	Third World	Mean total
1954	42	6	53	27
1958	43	5	52	27
1962	45	8	51	22
1966	43	8	49	23
1970	38	7	55	27
1974	33	10	57	30
1978	32	9	59	35
1982	32	8	61	37

terms the OECD receives substantial positive priority. We check, in simple terms, for any possible relation of diplomatic ties by bloc to military expenditure and find none.[37] This is due primarily to the fact that while Third World countries do display some variation in relative preference, the variation in the absolute number of embassies is greater than any variation in relative preference across blocs.[38]

As far as trade is concerned we see, from Table 5.8, over time a slight decline in the relative importance of the OECD and an increase both for COMECON and the Third World. Nonetheless, even by 1982 the OECD countries dominate Third World trade, the Third World comes a poor second, while the COMECON share is close to negligible.[39] The USA and USSR enjoy approximately equal positions of importance within each of their respective blocs, with neither being in a dominant position. We can find no systematic relation between bloc trade and military expenditure, which we attribute primarily to the overwhelming importance of the OECD bloc.[40]

In the area of arms imports, though Table 5.9 shows a decline of the OECD bloc over time in favour of the COMECON bloc, the former still enjoys a dominant position. Though Third World arms exports are increasing they are nonetheless verging on the negligible.[41] Roughly speaking COMECON and the Third World exchange places on arms exports compared to trade. The USSR enjoys almost a monopoly position within its bloc which is quite different from the much less dominant position of the USA within the OECD. In arms exports the USSR comes close to rivalling the USA, which again differs radically from the trade picture. Again we can find little evidence that the source of arms has any influence on military expenditure.[42]

Table 5.8: Percentage of countries conducting categorized percentages of their exports to and imports from the OECD, USA, COMECON, USSR and Third World, 1954, 1966,1982

% countries by year and bloc		Categorized % of exports/imports				
		0	1–25	26–50	51–75	76–100
1954	OECD	0/0	4/0	13/4	25/32	58/64
	USA	4/0	46/48	17/8	13/32	21/12
	COMECON	75/64	25/36	0/0	0/0	0/0
	USSR	80/96	20/4	0/0	0/0	0/0
	3W	0/0	63/64	21/32	13/4	4/0
1966	OECD	0/0	6/0	10/5	28/45	57/49
	USA	10/0	60/66	21/30	8/4	1/0
	COMECON	42/36	56/64	3/1	0/0	0/0
	USSR	63/64	36/34	1/1	0/0	0/0
	3W	1/0	68/66	19/32	7/3	4/0
1982	OECD	0/0	4/0	22/20	45/56	27/24
	USA	10/0	57/74	24/22	6/4	2/0
	COMECON	31/34	67/66	2/0	0/0	0/0
	USSR	48/68	48/32	2/0	0/0	0/0
	3W	0/0	43/28	37/56	14/14	4/0

Table 5.9: Percentage of countries conducting categorized percentages of their arms imports from the OECD, USA, COMECON, USSR and Third World, 1954, 1966,1982

% countries by year and bloc		Categorized % of arms imports				
		0	1–25	26–50	51–75	76–100
1954	OECD	24	0	0	0	76
	USA	52	12	8	0	28
	COMECON	100	0	0	0	0
	USSR	100	0	0	0	0
	3W	100	0	0	0	0
1966	OECD	32	5	4	3	55
	USA	57	5	9	5	24
	COMECON	86	0	1	3	11
	USSR	87	1	0	1	11
	3W	96	4	0	0	0
1982	OECD	17	12	0	9	62
	USA	48	17	12	3	19
	COMECON	83	7	0	0	10
	USSR	85	5	0	0	10
	3W	60	24	9	0	7

Summary

Measured across a number of varied and important areas, covering trade, investment, diplomatic ties and arms imports, Third World international interactions have expanded substantially in the postwar period not only in absolute but more importantly in relative terms. Taking the variables of international interaction as measures of international activity, we find that Third World countries in aggregate have displayed an increased propensity to international activity. In this sense we may argue that Third World countries have become more integrated into the international system.

Though the developments both of the expansion of the international system, brought about through Third World independence, and of the propensity to increasing international activity represent important changes in the structure of the international system, these developments have not radically transformed the dynamics of the system. Thus, while South–South interactions have increased (especially in diplomatic terms, less so in trade and hardly at all in arms imports and investment) as have South–East interactions (especially in arms imports, rather less so in diplomatic ties, still less in trade and not at all in investment) at the expense of the West, Western dominance has hardly been dented. The single most important reason for the absence of any radical change is that Third World countries have joined as very unequal partners an international system in which the major parameters of interaction had already been established and could easily continue to be controlled and dominated by the West. The growth of Third World international activity has, in other words, taken place in an international system in which the broad lines of inequality have remained essentially unchanged.

This descriptive profile sets the background from which the principal concern of this chapter is derived. The immediate objective, as defined in our general working hypothesis, is to examine the nature of the relationship of international interactions and military expenditure. More generally we take the variables profiling international interactions to be operational measures of international activity, and as such necessary though not sufficient indicators of international integration, while military expenditure is taken to be an operational measure of nation-state silence.

The rationale underpinning the examination of this relationship is developed from our contention that the nature of this relationship figures prominently in the schools of thought known loosely as idealism and realism. Both idealism and realism have a similar interest in, and attach a similar importance to, the relationship of international activity and nation-state salience in their mutual conviction that this relationship is central to an explanation of competition and conflict and therefore crucial to prescriptions for conflict management. The difference between these two schools of thought centres on differing perceptions of the source of conflict and thereby on the form of management. This difference in turn is neatly captured by the different form of the relationship of international activity to nation-state salience.

For the idealist the existence of competitive sovereign states is a major source of potential conflict. The promotion of international interaction thereby becomes a strategy whereby in effect the concentration of power inherent in sovereign states can be shattered. The goal for the idealist then is to promote interaction as a means of creating a greater degree of decentralized pluralism. For the realist such decentralized pluralism, far from being a solution, is in fact the source of problems. The international system is taken inevitably to be decentralized but this decentralization needs to be managed not through diffusion but concentration of power. More especially it is the responsibility of states very consciously protecting their sovereign autonomy that lies at the heart of the various mechanisms that realists hold to be crucial for the management of international order. The erosion of nation state salience in other words would represent the erosion of the very actors that are responsible for order.

This debate is not confined either purely to academic 'theorizing', but in a slightly different guise has figured prominently in preoccupations voiced by Third World leaders. Initial enthusiasm with the success of decolonization and the granting of formal legal independence soon evaporated with the claim that integration in an international system of unequals was not conferring a *de facto* sovereignty on Third World states commensurate with their *de jure* sovereignty. A classic illustration of this reaction can be seen in the demands in the 1970s for a New International Economic Order, a set of demands that were voiced precisely to enhance *de facto* sovereignty. Taking increased military expenditure to be a means whereby *de facto* sovereignty could be enhanced, we would expect, other things being equal, that Third World leaders would not follow the idealist line but rather react to higher levels of international activity by expanding their military capabilities.

Our findings show no evidence that higher levels of international activity are associated with lower levels of military expenditure. While the absence of inverse relationships is quite clear, the evidence of positive relationships is varied. Both investment and trade appear to be unrelated to military expenditure, while trade diversification, diplomatic associations and especially arms imports are positive predictors of levels of military expenditure. From these results we draw the following implications.

First, international activity and nation state salience are not antithetical processes. Certainly in a Third World context, therefore, the growth of the former does not entail an erosion of the latter. In this respect the capacity for state adaptation, as envisaged by realism, seems decidedly more appropriate than the erosion, envisaged by idealism.

Second, though we find no corroboration for a prediction from the idealist perspective, we would argue that this does not constitute a rejection of idealism. There are at least two important sets of considerations, which we may think of as auxiliary hypotheses, that would explain why a liberal or idealist relationship may be accurate even though we can find no corroboration. The first of these is that international activity may well erode nation-state salience but that such erosion will only take place once international activity has developed to a level of intensity which it has not yet reached. Second, it must be recalled that we are dealing only with Third World countries and as such only with a particular sector of the international system. To the extent that Third World countries are influenced by the more developed countries, then a critical factor that could influence the failure of the erosion effect in the Third World is that this process has not developed in the high-income countries. While considerations such as these would inhibit us from rejecting the idealist position, it is the case that we cannot find any corroboration for it.

Turning from a focus on the absence of any inverse relationships, we consider in our third implication the consequences of the mixed evidence of both the null and positive relations. The most general observation is that there is clearly no generalized or blanket activity or integration effect on military expenditure. This conclusion we now elaborate in several points.

First, there seems no evidence to indicate consequently what we might term a capitalist integration effect. It seems entirely legitimate to us to think of our set of interaction variables as constituting a capitalist syndrome. These interactions have not only been originated by high-income countries but also strongly dominated by them, and especially by the West. We would, however, at the minimum have expected a more generalized effect (i.e. indications of a positive relationship from all the interaction variables) than we actually find. If there were to be some variation in positive influence, since we would not require generalization to entail total uniformity, we would have expected the stronger positive influences to come from investment and trade associations on the grounds that these variables more closely and directly operationalize the principal components of capitalist diffusion. These variables, however, are the ones that have the weakest effect. Furthermore, though there would be some dangers in exaggerating the point, there are no signs of a specifically Western effect.

Second, it would seem to be the case that Third World political leaders do not respond to preoccupations about threats to *de facto* sovereignty by increasing military expenditure. The preoccupation with a misfit between *de jure* and *de facto* sovereignty does appear to be a very real one and again we would have expected the *de facto* problems to be generalized. Our findings do not of course indicate that preoccupations with *de facto* sovereignty do not exist but they do indicate that enhancing military expenditure is not regarded as an appropriate response.

Third, we are obliged to think of the impact of international activity in selective or variable terms. In other words international activity is not a unidimensional phenomenon. Those measures of international interaction which are most immediately economic and private, namely those interactions covering trade and investment, appear to be relatively autonomous from military expenditure. On the other hand, those interactions which have a stronger politico-economic and state content, namely trade diversification, diplomatic ties and arms imports, do have a positive effect on military expenditure. Consequently we see military expenditure, at least in part, as a positive response on the part of Third World governments to a heightened international political awareness and susceptibility to a political demonstration effect, which is especially pronounced in an imported military–industrial complex.

In sum, international activity most assuredly does not seem to be undermining nation-state salience, at least as we measure this in one of its principal manifestations, namely military expenditure. On the other hand, we equally cannot find any stimulative effect on military expenditure coming through any generalized international syndrome, as profiled, for instance, in the diffusion of capitalism. Rather the positive effect we do find appears to be rather more selective and to be tied principally to state managed politico-economic interactions. Higher levels of international activity, when those levels reflect state activity, far from undermining appear to enhance nation-state salience.

Notes

1. Both realism and idealism (which we take to be generally speaking synonymous with liberalism) represent complex bodies of thought to which we cannot do justice in any brief presentation. For a more detailed outline of the complexities and variations which might be said to define realism and liberalism, see: I. Clark, *Reform and Resistance in the International Order* (London: Cambridge University Press, 1980); R.D. McKinlay and R. Little, *Global Problems and World Order* (London: Pinter, 1986).

2. For a varied sample selection of writings that broadly can be characterized as realist, see: H. Bull, *The Anarchical Society* (New York: Columbia University Press, 1977); E.H. Carr, *The Twenty Years Crisis* (London: Macmillan, 1981); J.H. Herz, *Political Realism and Political Idealism* (Chicago: University of Chicago Press, 1951); J.H. Herz, *International Politics in the Atomic Age* (New York: Columbia University Press, 1959); S.D. Krasner, *Defending the National Interest* (Princeton: Princeton University Press, 1978); H. Morgenthau, *Politics Among Nations* (New York: Knopf, 1948); R.W. Tucker, *The Inequality of Nations* (London: Martin Robertson, 1977).

3. For a varied sample, see: N. Angell, *The Great Illusion* (London: Heinemann, 1911); J.W. Burton, *International Relations* (Cambridge: Cambridge University Press, 1967); J.W. Burton, *Peace Theory* (New York: Knopf, 1962); I. Claude, *Swords into Ploughshares* (London: London University Press, 1965); R.A. Falk, *The Promise of World Order* (Brighton: Wheatsheaf, 1987); D. Mitrany, *A Working Peace System* (Chicago: Quadrangle Books, 1966); O. Palme, *Common Security* (London: Pan, 1982).

4. For a varied selection, see: L.R. Brown, *World Without Borders* (New York: Viking, 1973); J.W. Burton, *World Society* (Cambridge: Cambridge University Press, 1972); R.O. Keohane and J. Nye (eds), *Transnational Relations and World Politics* (Cambridge: Harvard University Press, 1972); G. Mally, *Interdependence* (Lexington, D.C. Heath, 1976); E.L. Morse, 'The Transformation of Foreign Policies', *World Politics*, 22, 3, 1969; E.L. Morse, 'Transnational Economic Processes', *International Organization*, 25, 3, 1971; H. Sprout and M. Sprout, *Towards a Politics of the Planet Earth* (New York: Van Nostrand, 1971).

5. For a selection, see: D.P. Calleo, 'The Postwar Atlantic System and its Future', in E.O. Czempiel and D.A. Rustow (eds), *The Euro-American System* (Frankfurt: Campus-Verlag, 1976); R. Gilpin, 'The Politics of Transnational Economic Relations', *International Organization*, 25, 3, 1971; J.N. Rosenau, 'Adaptive Politics in an Interdependent World', *Orbis*, 16, 1, 1972; K.N. Waltz, 'The Myth of National Interdependence', in C.P. Kindleberger (ed.), *The International Corporation* (Cambridge: MIT Press, 1970).

6. It should be emphasized that while our hypothesis has the interesting hallmarks of a critical experiment (in that two bodies of thought make opposing predictions), we do not regard our hypothesis as constituting a critical experimental test of idealism and realism. Both 'theories', or schools of thought as we would prefer to label them, are far too complex and, in our view, confused to be evaluated in terms of a single hypothesis critical test.

7. The relationship, we reason, between international interaction and military expenditure is in this context something of a generalized or indirect one. There are more direct means by which states can manage international interactions, as for example by government controls over trade. Thus we do not reason that interaction explicitly triggers or stimulates a counter-response of military expenditure. Rather we posit that the maintenance of military expenditure even in the face of high levels of interaction is indicative of an expression on the part of states that such interaction does not portend their transformation.

8. Investment income and foreign direct investment figures are taken from the IMF *Balance of Payments Yearbook*. It is unfortunately only possible to obtain factor income figures in net form, i.e. as the balance of earnings of foreigners inside a country and of that country's nationals overseas. Ideally we would like only the former figure. While it is generally the case that net factor income from abroad will be negative for Third World countries, a net figure of zero could be achieved because of high earning both on the part of foreigners and of that country overseas. Consequently care has to be exercised in interpreting net factor income as a measure of foreign penetration. Figures are taken from the IMF *Financial Statistics*.

9. Figures are taken from the UN *Yearbook of International Trade Statistics* and IMF *Financial Statistics*. The diversification indices are calculated using the Gini-Hirschman index.

10. Figures are taken from the *Europa Yearbook* and *Statesman's Yearbook*.

11. Figures are taken from files kindly made available by the Stockholm International Peace Research Institute.

12. For a sample selection of these competing positions, see on the one hand: R.C. Amacher *et al.* (eds), *Challenges to a Liberal International Economic Order* (Washington: American Enterprise Institute, 1979); P.T. Bauer, *Dissent on Development* (London: Weidenfeld & Nicolson, 1971); F. McFadzean *et al.*, *Towards an Open World Economy* (London: Macmillan, 1972); see on the other hand: S. Amin, *Unequal Development* (London: Monthly Review Press, 1976); S. Amin, *Imperialism and Unequal Development* (London: Monthly Review Press, 1977); R.J. Barnet and R.E. Muller, *Global Reach* (London: Cape, 1975); A.G. Frank, *On Capitalist Underdevelopment* (Bombay: Oxford University Press, 1975); E. Mandel, *Late Capitalism* (London: New Left Books, 1976).

13. The bivariate correlations of military expenditure to both investment income and foreign direct investment are highly significant. The correlations generally increase a little over time, averaging respectively for investment income and foreign direct investment 0.60 and 0.57 over our eight test years. (Incidentally the two variables themselves show high correlations indicating a propensity for higher levels of new investment to flow proportionately to countries yielding higher investment income.) In trying to predict – in regression tables from these variables – military expenditure once GDP is controlled, neither variable ever appears as a significant positive estimator. In four of our eight test years, one or other of the variables appears as a weak negative estimator controlling for GDP. This would not, incidentally, support

some of the *dependencia* ideas that foreign direct investment in Third World countries is secured by an elite of which the military is seen as a dominant part.

14. The proportion with positive balances increases slightly over time from, for example, 7 per cent in 1958 to 15 per cent in 1978.

15. Plotting military expenditure against a horizontal axis representing net factor income we would expect a 'V' relationship centring on a balance of zero. If we took absolute values for net factor income, i.e. removed the sign, we would therefore expect to find positive correlations with military expenditure. This we do with average correlations over our eight test years being 0.59. However, once we control for GDP, which we can see most easily from the correlations of relative military expenditure to the absolute value of net factor income as a percentage of GDP, the correlations become insignificant. It could be argued that the 'V' may have different slopes for positive and negative values and may not meet at a point. This we could test by regressing military expenditure on GDP, the absolute value of net factor income, a dummy for the sign and an interaction term. These equations do not yield significant estimators.

16. There are no signs in other words for an inverted 'V' relationship.

17. The easiest way to see this is to look at correlations between relative military expenditure and a dummy representing a positive balance. This produces a small but significant correlation in five of six test periods from 1962 onwards (averaging over the six tests 0.36). There are also significant correlations between relative military expenditure and percentage net factor income (the sign is reinserted after the variable has been logged). There is not, however, a continuous relationship which we know from the absence of any significant association between relative military expenditure and percentage absolute net factor income. This relationship is purely a reflection of the dummy effect, and consequently slightly weaker (averaging 0.30), and therefore misleading.

18. Part of the difficulties we face with this investigation of net factor income may well pertain to its measurement. Ideally we would like to look at the positive and negative components separately, but figures are not available. Consequently a country may have a net balance which approximates to zero while having large foreign production both inside its borders and overseas which are approximately equal. Net factor income does not therefore directly predict to international interaction but to the balance on such interaction.

19. For the sake of interest we include in Table 5.1 descriptive statistics on export diversification by commodity, though we do not use this variable in our analysis. It is again measured using the Gini-Hirschman index with the UN Standard International Trade Classification as the way of classifying commodities.

20. The acronyms in Tables 5.2 and 5.2(A) are: IL (International Liquidity), E (Exports), M (Imports), DIVED (Diversification of Exports by Destination), DIVMS (Diversification of Imports by Source), PE (Exports as Percentage of GDP-logged).

21. The acronyms in Table 5.3 are: EMBTOT (Total Embassies Accredited by), EMTTOT (Total Embassies Accredited to), DIVED (Diversification of Exports by Destination), DIVMS (Diversification of Imports by Source), PE (Exports as a Percentage of GDP-logged), PM (Imports as a Percentage of GDP-logged).

22. The slight drop in the early 1960s represents a large number of African countries reaching independence and taking a few years to begin to establish their diplomatic networks.

23. The correlations, significant at the 0.05 level or beyond, are 0.31 (EMTTOT, 1962); 0.36 (EMTTOT, 1966); 0.32 (EMTTOT, 1970); 0.34 (EMTTOT, 1974).

24. Our means of measuring diplomatic ties yields a strange mix between a relative and gross measure. It is gross in the sense that we measure an absolute number, but relative in that it does not take account of embassy size. This strange mixture accounts, we suspect, for why it predicts to relative military expenditure, which other things being equal we would not expect to be sensitive to pure absolute variables. It would have made little sense to 'relativize' it by, say, dividing it by population size as we would envisage that otherwise similar small and large countries would differ not in number of embassies but size of embassies. Ideally therefore we would have liked to weight number of embassies by embassy size to yield a better absolute measure and then divide this by population size to give a better relative measure. It is, however, impossible to gain this data without such an attempt becoming a project in its own right.

25. Referring back to Table 5.2, we now have nicer equations for absolute military expenditure in 1974 and 1978. They are:

$$1974 \quad : 0.41 \text{ (GDP)} + \quad 0.43 \text{ (E)} \qquad -0.01 \text{ (DIVMS)}$$
$$(0.31) \qquad\qquad (0.35) \qquad\qquad (-0.17)$$
$$+0.01 \text{ (EMBTOT)} \quad R^2 = 0.85$$
$$(0.26)$$

$$1978 \quad : 0.56 \text{ (M)} + \quad 0.32 \text{ (IL)} \qquad -0.01 \text{ (DIVED)}$$
$$(0.45) \qquad\qquad (0.34) \qquad\qquad (-0.14)$$
$$+ 0.01 \text{ (EMTTOT)} \quad R^2 = 0.85$$
$$(0.15)$$

Referring back to Table 5.2(A), we have nicer equations for relative military expenditure for 1966 and 1970. They are:

$$1966 \quad : -0.01 \text{ (DIVED)} + 0.01 \text{ (EMBTOT)}$$
$$(-0.23) \qquad\qquad\qquad (0.28)$$
$$+ 0.28 \text{ (PIL)} \qquad R^2 = 0.27$$
$$(0.25)$$

$$1970 \quad : -0.02 \text{ (DIVMS)} + 0.01 \text{ (EMTTOT)} \qquad R^2 = 0.25$$
$$(-0.39) \qquad\qquad\qquad (0.23)$$

26. We do not subscribe to some of the more extreme military industrial complex arguments that this complex is the sole determinant of military developments. Nonetheless we do agree with the position that a military industrial complex (extended by some writers to include an academic dimension) not only actively underwrites the military system as a whole but has strong interests in promoting the continuous development of weapons systems. For some varied discussion see: R.J. Barnet, *The Economy of Death* (New York: Atheneum, 1970); S. Melman (ed.), *The War Economy of the United States* (New York: St Martin's Press, 1971); S. Melman, *The Permanent War Economy* (New York: Simon and Schuster, 1974); G. Prins *et al.*, *Defended to Death* (Harmondsworth: Penguin, 1983); S.C. Sarkesian (ed.), *The Military–Industrial Complex* (Beverley Hills: Sage, 1971).

27. Without wishing to put words in the mouths of others, the types of arguments we are making here have been made consistently by the Stockholm International Peace Research Institute (SIPRI). From its first major study (SIPRI, *The Arms Trade with the Third World* (London: Paul Elek, 1971)), research has been sustained and reported in

the annual Yearbooks, and has most recently been reported in a very detailed and comprehensive study (M. Brzoska and T. Ohlson, *Arms Transfers to the Third World 1971–85* (Oxford: Oxford Unversity Press, 1987)). For more general discussions of the interdependence inherent in modern weapons systems, see e.g. S.J. Deitchman, *New Technologies and Military Power* (Boulder: Westview, 1979); M. Janowitz, *The Professional Soldier* (New York: Free Press, 1960); M. Kaldor, *The Baroque Arsenal* (London: Deutsch, 1982); H. York, *Race to Oblivion* (New York: Simon and Schuster, 1970).

28. The mean value of arms imports in constant prices are: 54 (1954), 62 (1958), 44 (1962), 51 (1966), 102 (1970), 144 (1974), 238 (1978), and 282 (1982).

29. The reason for this is that a number of countries do not import arms. The percentage of cases not receiving arms imports are: 24 (1954), 14 (1958), 28 (1962), 28 (1966), 32 (1970), 29 (1974), 17 (1978), 14 (1982).

30. There are significant equations (with the dummy also being significant) for the absolute military expenditure equations for each of our test years from 1962 to 1982 and for the relative military expenditure equations from 1958 to 1982.

31. Since the dummy is of course not logged, the b coefficient is simply added in the logged equation to the constant term. The antilog of the b coefficient then indicates the proportionate increase in the dependent variable produced by the presence of the dummy. The proportionate increases for relative military expenditure are: 2.5 (1958), 2.6 (1962), 1.9 (1966), 2.1 (1970), 1.7 (1974), 2.6 (1978), and 2.3 (1982) giving an average of 2.2. For relative military expenditure the regressions are equivalent to a simple difference of means test.

32. These are the equations that have been used above and reported in Tables 5.2 and 5.2(A). The potential list of estimators on which stepwise regressions are run comprise: GDP, per capita GDP, exports (gross and percentage), imports (gross and percentage), international liquidity (gross and percentage), export and import diversification, and the dummy.

33. The dummy appears as a significant estimator for gross military expenditure in the 1970 and 1978 test years and for relative military expenditure in the 1958, 1966, 1970 and 1978 test years.

34. Following our general use of logs, low is defined as 1–10, medium 11–100, and high 101 plus. The dummy for low is defined as 1 for all cases falling in the 1–10 range with all other cases coded as zero, and likewise for the other categories. Consequently zero recipients are defined by the constant term, while any other category is the constant term plus the appropriate b coefficient, which in turn therefore indicates in its antilogged form the proportionate increase produced by that category. The acronyms used for these levels are: AI1, AI2, AI3 representing respectively low, medium and high levels of arms imports.

35. The different levels of arms imports are forced into the equation. Consequently our interest centres critically on the significance or otherwise of each categorized level.

36. While other things being equal we would expect the categorized levels to predict to absolute military expenditure better than the dummy equations (which is always the case), this of course need not hold unless there is a significant arms effect when other variables are introduced into the equation (in particular the size effect is removed). The results for relative military expenditure are rather interesting in that we are regressing a relative on an absolute variable. Admittedly the absolute variable has been simplified into an ordinal one but regressions substituting a logged measure of arms imports (excluding the zero recipients) produce much the same results. We

cannot, due to the measurement system of arms imports, relativize arms imports by expressing them as a percentage of GDP. The significant equations for relative military expenditure point in particular to a volume effect rather than a relative effect of arms imports. Thus two countries of different GDP importing the same volume of arms will move to the same relative military expenditure score even though the relative magnitude of the arms imports to GDP must be different. This in turn means, comfortingly, that we are not simply measuring a given addition to relative military expenditure for a given proportion of arms over GDP.

37. We correlate number of embassies which each bloc against military expenditure and look for any variations in the strength of these relations that might indicate a bloc influence. The correlations show little variation. In 1978 and 1982 for example correlations of total embassies accredited by Third World countries to all other states are 0.73 and 0.67, which compares with correlations of 0.71 and 0.66 (to other Third World countries), 0.70 and 0.63 (to the OECD) and 0.45 and 0.40 (to COMECON) – the latter is smaller simply due to the smaller number of countries. Correlations of percentage of embassies with relative military expenditure again show no significant variation.

38. The best way to measure this is to focus on the coefficient of variation, i.e. the standard deviation divided by mean, to control for an expected increase in variation as mean size increases. The coefficients of variation for all embassies accredited to other states are in 1978 and 1982: 0.56 and 0.55, compared with 0.15 and 0.15 (for Third World countries), 0.27 and 0.28 (for OECD countries) and 0.63 and 0.67 (for COMECON). There is certainly greater variation across Third World countries in attention paid to the COMECON bloc, but again the numbers are sufficiently small to inhibit any systematic effect.

39. Table 5.8 profiles trade share. It could be the case that countries, say, enjoying large trade share with the OECD are small traders. Thus, while Table 5.8 would accurately profile bloc importance in frequency terms, it may misrepresent bloc importance in total trade. It does not. In 1982, for example, Third World exports to the OECD are three times those to Third World countries and forty times those to COMECON. The USA imports from and exports to the Third World 12 and 13 times the respective figures for the COMECON bloc as a whole and 21 and 51 times the respective figures for the USSR.

40. Simple correlations between bloc trade and military expenditure show little variation. Thus in 1978 and 1982 total exports of Third World countries correlate 0.87 and 0.86 with military expenditure. Analogous figures for the OECD, the Third World and COMECON are 0.70 and 0.72, 0.81 and 0.79, and 0.37 and 0.32. The lower associations for COMECON we attribute to low trade scores. Equally trade share with relative military expenditure shows no real variation. In 1978 and 1982 the correlations are –0.24 and –0.12 (OECD), 0.14 and 0.01 (Third World) and –0.02 and 0.02 (COMECON).

41. Again we profile, as with trade, arms import share. In aggregate terms OECD arms exports are 2½ times those of COMECON and 10 times those of the Third World.

42. This is not true in our early test years when the USSR had little or no arms exports and when in fact a dummy for US arms exports predicted slightly better to military expenditure than a dummy for OECD arms exports. This difference has reduced as the USSR has become a major exporter, though there is something of a continuing tendency for OECD arms exports to predict more strongly than COMECON ones to military expenditure.

6   Military Expenditure and Domestic Conflict

Introduction

Several general utilities are conventionally associated with the military, indicating thereby that the military should be understood as a multifaceted phenomenon. One of these facets is the role played by the military as a defining attribute of the state. The kind of themes explored in the earlier chapters, dealing with power capabilities and international interactions, draw heavily on this facet, thereby pointing to military utilities in the areas of power, status and prestige. Another conventional utility associated with the military pertains to the role of the military in conflict or conflict-related areas.

This and the subsequent chapters explore the relationships, respectively in domestic and interstate arenas, of conflict and conflict-related issues to military expenditure. The domestic focus of this chapter explores two main issue areas, of which the first falls under what we have termed conflict-related.

The point of departure for the rationale that underpins our general working hypothesis in the conflict-related area begins from a body of research defined in terms of its use as a bureaucratic politics perspective. In its commitment at the most general level to explicate the policy process, the bureaucratic politics perspective has yielded three important arguments of direct interest to us. These three arguments, which we do not pretend constitute a full review of this rich and complex area of investigation, may be summarized in terms of bureaucratic control, bureaucratic content and the bureaucratic dynamic.[1]

As far as control is concerned, it seems to be beyond dispute that bureaucratic influence on the policy process is substantial. This influence, furthermore, has been shown to be important at all levels of policy-making from initiation, to selection, to formulation, to implementation, as bureaucrats, for example, control the gathering and processing of information, or play a role in policy appraisal, or amend policies in the implementation stage.

Second, and perhaps more interestingly, research has documented what we might call a bureaucratic content influence. This content influence derives from the argument that bureaucracies display a major commitment to self-maintenance or expansion. This commitment works both at an individual level, due to preoccupations with job interest or security or promotion prospects, and at an organizational level, due to more collective concerns with the survival of the organization as a whole. The content influence manifests itself in a host of ways.

For example, it has been argued that bureaucracies have a propensity for low-risk policies, in order to decrease the probability of failure, or for policies that entail rapid expenditure, in order that future budgets can be justified. Or again, the propensity for bureaucracies, under contracting budgets, to cut services rather than line positions has been explained in terms of bureaucrats pursuing job protection. Yet again, the generally relatively low attention devoted to policy evaluation has been explained in part by bureaucrats being more preoccupied with the initiation and expenditure on projects rather than with the impact of projects.

The third argument derives from the investigation of bureaucratic interactions where it is suggested that the interactions produce a kind of self-sustaining dynamic that drives policy. Policy, in other words, is not simply a function in part of the influence of autonomous bureaucracies but also of interactions between them. The research in this general area most directly relevant to our concerns is the analysis of the influence of inter-service rivalry on weapons procurement and funding.[2]

Collectively these arguments provide strong evidence for a bureaucratic influence on policy. This body of evidence has then been applied to the study of public expenditure where a bureaucratic politics influence has been translated into an explanation of the behaviour of levels of expenditure. In other words, bureaucratic pressure and momentum are seen as driving forces that both predict and explain public expenditure. Corroboration of this is derived from the high correlations that are to be found across a range of different expenditure areas of one year's expenditure level to the next.[3]

We do not dispute this predictive ability. Nor do we dispute the interesting body of research produced from the bureaucratic politics perspective. We would, however, contend that this approach is generally speaking most useful in describing and explaining micro aspects of the policy process and decidedly less useful when employed at a more macro and comparative level. In particular, we are not happy with the translation of bureaucratic pressure and momentum into an explanation of the behaviour of expenditure levels.

The high correlations of one year's expenditure level to the next we take to be clear confirmation only of a descriptive prediction rather than an explanation. Adequate explanation requires not only successful prediction but also a satisfactory rationale, which we find to be somewhat lacking on two grounds. First, it would seem to us erroneous to pretend that governments maintain education or health or military expenditures simply to support the appropriate bureaucracies. It would seem rather to be the case that function explains organization rather than vice versa. Second, the bureaucratic pressure and momentum explanation is, in our view, either very superficial or little more than a tautology. To explain one year's level of spending by the previous year's does rather beg the question of what explains that year's. Or again, bureaucratic politics does not really help us to explain why a country may have say higher levels of military as opposed to say education expenditure, except to say rather tautologically that one has a larger bureaucracy than the other. Furthermore, it does not helpfully explain different commitment levels across countries except to say yet again that one would have a relatively larger bureaucracy than the other.

There is, however, one circumstance particularly relevant to our concerns whereby a macro policy effect on expenditure could be posited. Returning to a micro level, it has been noted that bureaucracies, as far as expenditure profiles are concerned, compete extensively with each other in a context which, though not zero-sum, does have some zero-sum elements.[4] Thus, not only may the equivalent of a Treasury constrain other government bureaucracies but these other bureaucracies may compete against each other for a share in what they take to be a relatively fixed pie.[5] Furthermore, bureaucracies must compete, other things being equal, against politicians, who may well hold different interests and sets of preferences, which in turn are supported by substantial capabilities such as parties or popular support.

The military can be seen in one sense as a pressure group, albeit a pressure group with a privileged access to government, in the narrow sense, in that it constitutes one of the main bureaucracies of government, in the broader sense. Other things being equal, we might expect that as the scope of that privileged access increased, by for instance leading figures in a bureaucracy becoming members of the government (in the narrow sense), then the comparative advantage of that bureaucracy in its competitive struggles with other bureaucracies would increase and it would, following then the bureaucratic influence idea, be freer to expand its expenditure. Particularly through the phenomenon of the military regime, Third World countries provide us with a good opening to test this proposition.

On the grounds then that the macro level of bureaucratic pressure and momentum become most pronounced when an opportunity becomes available for a bureaucracy to exert a more direct influence on government, our general working hypothesis proposes that higher levels of direct military influence on government will predict to higher levels of military expenditure.[6]

The variables, deployed to test this hypothesis, are: military coup, military regime, and percentage of posts held by the military in the main executive body. A military coup is defined as an action in which the military is the prime mover and which involves either the implicit or explicit use of force leading to the deposition of one government, whether civilian or military, and its replacement by another, whether it be civilian or military. Attempted coups, which do not result in a change of government, and junta changes are ignored. A military regime is one which is established by a coup, in which the main executive post is held by a military person, and which endures for at least six months. The main executive is exactly what the name implies and is taken to be synonymous with what we have thus far called government in the narrow sense.[7]

Our second area of investigation looks explicitly at domestic conflict. Conflict is an inherent feature, in fact it is a defining characteristic, of any political system. Other things being equal, however, political systems develop a large and varied array of mechanisms and institutions such that conflict can be managed or accommodated without the resort to force. Since we know of no political system where forceful conflict is the norm, then conflict that encompasses force, the only type of conflict in which we are interested, would be seen by us consequently as abnormal. By abnormal we explicitly do not refer either to the frequency or the undesirability of conflict but rather to the fact that forceful conflict is not the conventional means of pursuing political objectives. As such we take domestic conflict, by which from hereon we mean forceful conflict, to be indicative of a breakdown in domestic political legitimacy.[8]

Other things being equal, domestic conflict may not be thought to be of immediate relevance to the military. Thus in formal terms, it might be argued that the military is an apolitical body whose primary function is to maintain the external sovereignty of the state, leaving problems associated with domestic conflict to the government and police. In this event we would expect domestic conflict to be independent of military expenditure.

Our general working hypothesis, however, does not postulate independence but rather that domestic conflict will predict positively to military expenditure. In so doing we work on the basis that the military will be used as a response to domestic conflict and that as it is so used military expenditure will increase, due either to problems of lack of fungibility of military capabilities from external to domestic conflicts or to an unwillingness to reduce external capabilities through domestic employment.

We elaborate now briefly on why we adopt the view that the military may be used in a response capacity. First, it seems unrealistic to us to regard any military organization as entirely apolitical. Even within the OECD countries the military is a very vigorous political actor whose politicking due to policy interdependence is not simply confined to military matters narrowly defined. The main constraint on Western militaries, which indubitably has massively narrowed their sphere of political activity, has been professionalization. Though professionalization has certainly been adopted in Third World country militaries, assuredly moving the majority of militaries well beyond the caudillo type of organization, it is nonetheless not nearly so highly developed on aggregate as in the West. The main import of lower developments of professionalization is that Third World militaries are decidedly prone to intervene in conflict situations either to protect their own positions or to support a particular regime or regime type.[9]

Second, the requisite that Third World militaries confine themselves to issues purely of external sovereignty seems to us highly unrealistic. In practice, internal and external sovereignty cannot always be easily separated. External sovereignty can be threatened both directly through, for example, secessionists movements, or indirectly, if domestic conflict is sufficiently acute, through civil wars. Even below this level it is entirely conceivable that Third World governments, which generally face very substantial problems in establishing domestic legitimacy, confront levels of violence with which they cannot cope solely by using a police force (even when that force contains a paramilitary wing). In this context it may be recalled that the use of the military in situations of domestic conflict within the OECD countries, which face massively lower legitimacy problems, though rather uncommon is certainly not unknown.

Turning to our measurements of domestic conflict, it is undoubtedly the case that our variables are, for rather obvious reasons, somewhat crude. Domestic conflict is initially measured as a dummy. Its presence requires that force or violence is explicitly used, that such force results in fatalities, and that the violence is geared toward some explicitly political goal.

The assessment of conflict is then refined somewhat by defining three more dummies. First, we distinguish organized and unorganized conflict, wherein the former conflict is perpetrated by an institutionalized group that has an explicit military wing. Second, we distinguish sporadic and sustained conflict, where sporadic is defined in terms either of time (which means at relatively isolated points in time) or of event (which means the events are relatively discrete). Finally, we distinguish regionalized and generalized conflict, where the former must both be confined to a region and have aspirations only for that region.[10]

Findings

Our first area of investigation centres on the domestic conflict related area which has been equated with direct military influence on government. Before examining whether such influence predicts to military expenditure, we note some rather interesting and relevant descriptive statistics.

From the data contained in Table 6.1 we draw three main conclusions. First, the military has played a rather active role in Third World governments. Averaging over our period of analysis, one in five Third World states is run at any one time by a military regime. Furthermore, although the figures are not neatly continuous, the relative frequency for Third World states to have military regimes is most certainly not decreasing. In fact our four test years from 1970 onwards show on average almost twice the proportion of military regimes as the average for the preceding four test years.

Table 6.1: Percentage frequency of Third World military regimes and of percentage of main executive positions held by the military, selected years 1954–82

Year	% frequency of military regime	% frequency of % executive positions held by the military				
		0–33	34–66	67–100	0–10	11–100
1954	13	97	3	0	62	38
1958	18	87	8	5	61	39
1962	11	94	5	2	71	29
1966	15	88	9	3	73	27
1970	24	87	11	2	61	39
1974	26	90	5	5	64	36
1978	33	81	10	10	57	43
1982	24	89	10	1	65	35

While we take one in five of all Third World governments being military to be an impressive display of direct governmental influence on the part of Third World militaries, our second conclusion argues that this display of direct influence is far from overwhelming. Two comments are in order. First, looking at the percentage of posts in the main executive held by the military, we see that on average the military holds 10 per cent or less of all executive positions in two-thirds of the countries. Or again, on average some 90 per cent of all countries, without very much variation over time, have executives in which the military hold less than a third of all executive positions. Second, military regimes show a substantial degree of civilianization. For instance, while the proportion of military regimes doubles over our second set of four test years, the percentage of executive posts has increased by only 50 per cent.[11] Or again, the proportion of countries displaying a military participation ratio in the executive of greater than two-thirds (all of which are cases of military regimes) constitutes a relatively small percentage even of military regimes. In fact, on average, only 15 per cent of military regimes have executive bodies in which the military holds two-thirds or more of the positions.

Our third conclusion is that the primary route to substantial participation of the military in the main executive body is through a military regime.[12] While it is certainly not the case that the only route to executive office is through a military regime, higher levels of military participation in the executive are generally contingent on a military regime. Thus, higher levels of military participation, which are certainly not the norm, are not distributed evenly across countries or within countries over time but are primarily concentrated in those periods during which countries experience a military regime. This means in turn, interestingly, that civilian regimes do not pander to the military by allocating the military a substantial share of executive positions.

We turn now to consider our regression results where we are hypothesizing that higher levels of direct influence by the military on government will lead to higher levels of military expenditure. The results show that we can find no evidence to indicate that direct military influence has any impact on military expenditure. While Third World states, compared at least with liberal democracies, are extremely vulnerable to military intervention, any such intervention does not carry in its wake any propensity for the military to develop any greater self-preference or priority by increasing its own spending power. Several elaborations and implications from this general result may be examined.

First, we find that the presence of a military regime does not predict to expenditure levels.[13] It may, very reasonably, be argued against this result that we have in the form of a dummy variable only a crude measure of influence. In the same line of critique it could also be argued, as we have in fact documented, that military influence does not of necessity presuppose a military regime or that military regimes vary in their degree of civilianization which would also undermine to some extent the predictive power of a dummy variable. We would indeed up to a point accept these reservations, which in fact explains why we have included the variable of percentage of executive posts held by the military. If the argument that a military regime, for whatever of the above reasons, is an insensitive measure, then we would expect percentage of executive posts to predict to military expenditure. Although we try several different representations of this variable we still cannot find a significant prediction.[14]

Second, it might be argued that we do not see an effect because we are looking for the wrong one. Thus, it could be argued that it is not military regimes which increase military expenditure but rather civilian ones, that do so in order to buy off the threat of a military regime. If this were the case then our predictor variables would be significant negative estimators, which they are not. In this context it might also be recalled that there is no propensity for civilian regimes to buy off military intervention by providing the military with more extensive positions.

Third, a more sophisticated variant of the above argument might run that some civilian regimes pander to the military by maintaining high levels of expenditure and it is only those civilian regimes which do not do this that experience military coups. This argument would indeed be consonant with the results we have provided thus far. However, this argument would also need to predict therefore that coups took place in countries with lower levels of military expenditure. This is not the case.[15]

Fourth, this does not mean of course that military regimes do not increase military expenditure. It does mean, however, that military regimes are either no more prone to raise (or for that matter lower) military expenditure than civilian regimes and/or that if military regimes do increase military expenditure then they do not raise it to a level higher than we would expect it to be on the basis of the country's GDP.

Fifth, these results give us something of an insight into militarization. While there is a general consensus on the 'theoretical' meaning of this concept, usually it is taken to refer to the promulgation and extension of military values and norms throughout a society, there has been some confusion, for very good reasons, over operational measures of this concept. Generally in operational form, militarization is taken to be an increase in those variables that profile 'things military'. In this context many of our descriptive findings confirm an image of increasing militarization of the Third World. Thus, we have documented increases in military expenditure, in arms imports, in the proportionate frequency of military regimes and in the percentage of executive posts held by the military. These, however, are all aggregate trends and care must be taken with relationships between aggregate trends. In this particular instance we cannot find any significant association between militarization, defined as higher levels of commitment to military expenditure, and militarization, as defined by higher levels of direct military influence on government.

Finally, we take our results to confirm our general suspicion that the bureaucratic politics approach, though very instructive at a micro level, is not at all helpful in more macro levels of explanation. Even in that rather special circumstance where a military regime is established, in other words a situation where a particular bureaucracy achieves a very real comparative advantage over its fellow competitors, we can find no evidence to indicate that that bureaucracy systematically favours itself by awarding itself a greater allocation. Any notion of the 'selfish bureaucracy' does not seem appropriate to the military.[16]

Turning to our second area of investigation, we may note from Table 6.2, though it must be recalled that we have some reservations on the reliability of our figures, that politically oriented domestic conflict entailing fatalities is both fairly extensive across Third World countries and most certainly not reducing. From a reliability standpoint we are decidedly happier with the identification of both organized conflict and sustained conflict, both of which show a clearer increase.[17] Thus, for example, from the mid-1960s somewhere between a quarter and a third of all Third World countries contain an institutionalized group engaged in violent conflict through a distinctive military wing.

Table 6.2: Percentage frequencies of Third World countries experiencing no domestic conflict, unorganized v. organized conflict, and sporadic v. sustained conflict, selected years 1954–82

Year	Conflict status				
	No domestic conflict	Unorganized conflict	Organized conflict	Sporadic conflict	Sustained conflict
1954	73	14	14	14	14
1958	45	39	15	45	9
1962	66	16	18	26	8
1966	54	16	30	36	11
1970	56	15	30	31	14
1974	47	25	28	36	17
1978	38	33	29	42	20
1982	43	32	25	35	22

Our regression results yield three main findings. First, the simple occurrence of domestic conflict does not predict extensively to military expenditure. This is, in fact, no great surprise as we anticipate that only higher levels of domestic conflict would so predict.[18] Second, we do find more consistent, positive results when we test for higher levels of domestic conflict, as measured by occurrence of either organized or sustained conflict.[19] Third, given this result we test for both a combined and an interactive effect of organized and sustained conflict. Though we find no significant results for an interactive effect, the joint occurrence of both organized and sustained conflict does improve our results marginally.[20]

In keeping with the strategy we have pursued throughout this study, we now submit these results to critical scrutiny. There are without doubt some serious objections that could be raised, which we order into three main sets.

The first of these, while accepting our rationale and general working hypothesis, would argue that we have understated the real domestic conflict effect. This could occur under either of two different circumstances. First, it may be objected that we underestimate a real conflict effect due to the insensitivity of our crude and unreliable measurements. To a degree we would agree, quite frankly, that our measurements are crude, as dummies usually are, and that there are unquestionably reliability problems. As such, there is no doubt that a more extensive and sensitive array of variables would have been preferable. Nonetheless we have two responses. First, for the purpose for which we intend our variables, we would argue that dummy measurements are certainly not inappropriate. By this we mean that we have been working under the assumption, which seems to be corroborated, that only higher levels of domestic conflict would have on impact in military expenditure. Second, we are generally more concerned with problems of overstating an influence, an enduring difficulty in the social sciences due to collinearity problems, rather than understating an influence. Though again we would readily concede that, at the limit, understating means missing an influence, in which event there is a very real problem. A second source of understating, which in our view is more likely than measurement problems to result in missing an influence, is a 'crowding-out' effect. Imagine, for instance, that domestic conflict did indeed predict to military expenditure but say much less strongly than a variable such as interstate conflict, to which it was in turn unrelated. Interstate violence would therefore mask or crowd out a domestic conflict influence. We can, however, largely circumvent this problem by controlling for the influence of other variables, which in fact we do at a later stage. The problem will only remain if we have omitted a major influence to which domestic conflict is unrelated. This we hope, though we cannot be sure, is not the case.

A second set of criticisms might in contrast argue that we have misinterpreted our results. Such a position would accept that there is indeed a relationship between domestic conflict and military expenditure but that we have drawn the relationship in the wrong direction, namely that military expenditure does not respond to domestic conflict but vice versa. Such a view would be premised initially, we presume, on the assumption, with which we are in general agreement, that groups would commit themselves to violent protest when they perceive, rightly or wrongly, that other avenues of protest are unsuccessful. Consequently, increases in the size of the military would raise the level of violence in which it would be necessary to engage. Such an argument is entirely consistent with our results, and no statistical manipulation, essentially since we are not dealing with a statistical problem, can resolve the matter either way. While we may admittedly be wrong, our general view is that military expenditure would not predict positively to domestic violence. We regard the decision to employ domestic violence as being much more likely a function of the salience of the issue to the protesting group and the perceived exhaustion of alternative means of protest. That a group or groups would be more prone to employ violence because relative military expenditure is say 10 per cent as opposed to 5 per cent of GDP seems to us unlikely.[21]

A third set of criticisms is that we misrepresent the relationship of domestic conflict and military expenditure. Two scenarios may be raised of which the first could argue that military expenditure would have a deterrent effect on conflict. As in the case considered above, once again military expenditure is not seen as the response but as the predictor variable. Our hunch is that this is a much more likely scenario than military expenditure predicting positively to domestic conflict. A deterrent effect would hypothesize an inverse relationship, which we can evaluate and which is of course inconsistent with our findings. Furthermore, while a deterrent effect of state force on domestic conflict seems eminently plausible to us, we would imagine, other things being equal, that such an effect is much more likely to come through the police than the military. A second scenario is more complicated and would posit that there could be two different and distinctive relations. In some countries military expenditure could be, as we hypothesize, a response to domestic conflict, while in other countries domestic conflict would be a response to a deterrent influence. In this event the aggregate result, amalgamating all countries, would produce an insignificant relationship between military expenditure and domestic conflict, which of course is the outcome we find in some, albeit a minority, of the test years. This, however, seems unlikely to us on two grounds. First, though we could easily model this situation, in which sense there is in fact a statistical solution which would require nothing more than an interaction term, we cannot think of a variable that would categorize countries into two camps that would enable us then to model the two different relationships. Second, even though we cannot think of a differentiating variable, were there even to be one, it would have to be the case that the distribution of relative military expenditure on the dummy of domestic conflict showed at least some signs of bimodality on each of the values of the dummy variable. Our scatterplots show no sign of this.

In sum, we unquestionably have some reservations both about the strength of our results and our interpretation of those results. Nonetheless the results show significant effects in a majority of years even though the amount of variation explained by domestic conflict is not terribly large.[22] While having some qualms on interpretations, the most persuasive explanation to us is that military expenditure does respond positively to domestic conflict. This positive impact of domestic conflict on military expenditure is, however, confined to that population of Third World countries, approximately a quarter in any test year, experiencing higher levels of domestic conflict, where by higher we understand sustained or organized violence. In these countries, other things being equal, higher levels of domestic conflict more than double on average the military burden.[23] Those countries, manifesting lower levels of domestic conflict, cannot be distinguished from countries experiencing no conflict. Violent domestic conflict in other words is never a really powerful predictor of military expenditure and only at sustained or organized levels does it become a sufficient condition for a greater commitment to military expenditure.

Summary

The first of two major preoccupations of this chapter has centred on what we have termed direct governmental influence by the military, by which we mean military participation in the main executive body or the establishment of a military regime. Military influence on government is not of course confined purely to this level. Indeed there is no reason not to suppose that at the pressure group level military political activity is universal, and, as such, as prevalent in, say, the West as the Third World. We do, however, work on the basis that direct governmental influence is more powerful than pressure group influence. Direct governmental influence, though not unique to Third World countries, is decidedly more marked in these countries as compared, say, with the West. Not only is such influence rather prevalent but it also shows no real signs of diminishing.

Against this background our first general working hypothesis was that direct governmental influence would predict positively to higher levels of military expenditure. We can find no corroboration for this hypothesis, meaning that higher levels of direct governmental influence by the military do not stimulate military expenditure. Furthermore, several alternative explanations, which may 'hide' a real political influence of the military on military expenditure, do not seem viable. Thus, the relationship is not 'hidden' by, for example, civilian regimes buying off the military or military influence being exerted outside the context of a military regime. From this general result we draw three main implications.

First, though we have in general little sympathy for the degree of explanation brought by the bureaucratic politics model, as it is deployed at a macro, comparative level to explain expenditures, we did consider in the limiting case where a bureaucracy, in this instance the military, could command a degree of direct governmental influence, that a bureaucratic politics explanation could be of value. Our failure to produce significant positive results even in the limiting case corroborates our view that, while a focus on bureaucratic politics at the micro level is very fruitful and instructive, such a focus is singularly unhelpful in explaining variation in expenditure at a macro comparative level. The 'selfish' bureaucracy is not a sound model at a macro level.

Second, and somewhat as a corollary to the point above, we may learn something about the motivation underpinning Third World military political activity. We certainly do not wish to give the impression of Third World militaries as paragons of virtue. Though they certainly cannot be accused, from a human-rights perspective, of holding a monopoly on brutality, military regimes un-questionably can be brutal. Furthermore, even though generally speaking we subscribe to the position that military intervention is more a symptom than a cause of political instability, we also, again generally speaking, hold the view that military regimes cannot provide a substantial basis for more enduring stability. Nonetheless, on aggregate, it is quite clear that promotion of their own narrow interests, as measured by voting themselves greater resources, is most certainly not a primary motivation for Third World military political activity. In this respect Third World militaries display a marked degree of professionalization.

Finally, we may note that the process of militarization is certainly not uni-dimensional. Looking across the behaviour of a range of indicators that could be said to operationalize militarization, such as military expenditure, arms imports, military coups or military regimes, we may well infer from growth rates over time a cumulative process of militarization. In so doing we would, however, be incurring a major problem of misaggregation. These different facets of militarization are far from synchronized. Though it is rather important to note that these indicators generally show positive growth rates, their growth is not, across the board, mutually reinforcing.

The second major preoccupation of this chapter has been to examine the influence of domestic conflict on military expenditure. Though there are some undoubted data difficulties with the measurement of domestic conflict, we are moderately confident in asserting that high levels of domestic conflict are a prevalent and seemingly enduring characteristic of Third World states. On the grounds essentially that domestic violence can challenge not only the military's formal monopoly of legitimate force but also threaten either the viability of the state as a whole or the regime with which the military may identify, we have hypothesized that higher levels of domestic conflict will elicit a response of higher levels of military expenditure.

We do unquestionably have some qualms about both our results and our interpretation of the results. One counter hypothesis we can, however, reject with some confidence. That hypothesis is that larger militaries have a deterrent effect on domestic conflict. Certainly if Third World governments aspire to deter domestic conflict by developing their military capabilities, then that aspiration is not achieved.

We are less confident in rejecting a second interpretation, namely that larger militaries encourage domestic conflict to take a more violent form. We can well envisage that the military may be a critical object of conflict by virtue of its general political disposition or its affiliation with a particular government. In this respect the military could contribute to domestic conflict. While we accept this argument in principle, and indeed think it highly likely in practice, it does not seem to us to bear particularly on military expenditure. If the military were to be a source of conflict we consider that it would be the political disposition or affiliation of the military rather than its capabilities that would explain conflict. It does in fact seem unlikely to us that the size of the military would influence a decision to employ higher levels of conflict. Indeed were there to be a size effect we would expect that effect to be a deterrent rather than a stimulative one (and this we know not to be the case).

We are consequently inclined to accept some corroboration of our general working hypothesis. In so doing, two points may be noted. First, our findings are neither very powerful nor consistent across all years. The principle reason, we suspect, for this is that domestic groups engaging in violent conflict cannot in general match the capabilities of the military. In other words, military capabilities are on aggregate sufficiently large, other things being equal, that higher levels are not required to respond to domestic conflict. Second, though the findings are not very powerful, we do nonetheless have some significant results, which in turn means that military expenditure can and does respond to domestic conflict. Consequently, we infer that if domestic violence becomes sufficiently acute, as for instance by taking a sustained or organized form, it will be met with higher levels of military expenditure. We appear therefore to have a domestic illustration of how force begets force.

Notes

1. The literature on bureaucracy is legion. For a varied selection covering both reviews and original works, see: M. Albrow, *Bureaucracy* (London: Macmillan, 1970); G.T. Allison, *Essence of Decision* (Boston: Little Brown, 1971); D. Beetham, *Bureaucracy* (Milton Keynes: Open University Press, 1987); A. Breton and R. Wintrobe, *The Logic of Bureaucratic Conduct* (Cambridge: Cambridge University Press, 1982); A. Downs, *Inside Bureaucracy* (Boston: Little Brown, 1967); C.E. Lindblom, *The Policy Making Process* (Englewood Cliffs: Prentice Hall, 1968); R.K. Merton (ed.), *Reader in Bureaucracy* (New York: Free Press, 1952); R. Michels, *Political Parties* (New York: Free Press, 1962); E.C. Page, *Political Authority and Bureaucratic Power* (Brighton: Wheatsheaf, 1985); C. Perrow, *Organisational Analysis* (Belmost: Wadsworth, 1970); P. Self, *Administrative Theories and Politics* (London: Allen & Unwin, 1973).
2. See e.g. G. Allison and F. Morris, 'Armaments and Arms Control', *Daedalus*, CIV, 1975; C.S. Gray, *The Soviet–American Arms Race* (Westmead: Saxon House, 1976); R.C. Gray, 'Learning from History', *World Politics*, 31, 1979; J.R. Kurth, 'Why We Buy the Weapons We Do', *Foreign Policy*, 11, 1973; H.G. Mosley, *The Arms Race* (Lexington: Lexington Books, 1985); B. Russett, *The Prisoners of Insecurity* (San Francisco: Freeman, 1983).
3. In our area of interest, the military expenditure of any one state in any one year would be seen as being determined by the previous year's allocation. See also C.S. Gray, op. cit.
4. In the context of governmental bureaucracies the competition is non-zero sum in that the overall budget may expand. However, once a budget level is fixed then competition becomes zero-sum, i.e. one bureaucracy can gain only at the expense of another.
5. In this context the main thrust of the inter-service rivalry literature has not been used to explain aggregate levels of military expenditure so much as which branch of the armed forces gets how much.
6. For a sample of general reading on the subject matter of military coups and regimes, see: C.S. Clapham and G. Philip, *The Political Dilemmas of Military Regimes* (Beckenham: Croom Helm, 1985); J. van Doorn, *The Soldier and Social Change* (London: Sage, 1975); G. Kennedy, *The Military in the Third World* (London: Duckworth, 1974); S.E. Finer, *The Man On Horseback* (London: Penguin, 1976); M. Janowitz, *Military Institutions and Coercion in the Developing Nations*, (Chicago: Chicago University Press, 1977); M. Janowitz and J. van Doorn (eds), *On Military Intervention* (Rotterdam: Rotterdam University Press, 1971); R.H.T. O'Kane, *The Likelihood of Coups* (Aldershot: Avebury, 1987); E. Luttwak, *Coups d'Etat* (London: Wildwood House, 1979); S.W. Simon (ed.), *The Military and Security in the Third World* (Boulder: Westview, 1978).

7. There are undoubtedly reliability problems with these variables deriving not only from data availability but also from our classifications according to our definitions. Generally speaking, however, we are reasonably confident that for the type of measurement we make these problems are not too great. Military coups, given that we ignore failed ones, are relatively easy to identify, as indeed, consequently, are military regimes. The greatest difficulty with military regimes pertains more to their termination. Again they usually terminate (our criteria are an election or the main executive post passing to a civilian) in a relatively unambiguous manner but there are some cases where classification is hazy, and therefore potentially unreliable. As far as the executive is concerned, past and present military personnel are classed as military (there is a tendency for military titles to be dropped) unless the person has been elected. The main data sources are: *Keesings Contemporary Archives*, annual editions of the *Europa Yearbook*, annual editions of the *Statesman's Yearbook*, and editions of *Political Handbook and Atlas of the World*. By using all these sources, though we certainly cannot guarantee full reliability, we are satisfied that our measures achieve an appropriate level of reliability.

8. The literature on domestic conflict is truly vast. We make no pretence to summarize or order this literature. For two rather good overviews, see H. Eckstein, 'Theoretical Approaches to Explaining Collective Political Violence', in T.R. Gurr (ed.), *Handbook of Political Conflict* (New York: Free Press, 1980); E. Zimmerman, 'Macro Comparative Research on Political Protest', in ibid.

9. For general discussions, see: M.R. van Gils (ed.), *The Perceived Role of the Military* (Rotterdam: Rotterdam University Press, 1971); M. Janowitz, *The Professional Soldier* (New York: Free Press, 1960); M. Janowitz and J. van Doorn (eds), *On Military Ideology* (Rotterdam: Rotterdam University Press, 1971); A. Perlmutter (ed.), *Political Influence of the Military* (New Haven: Yale University Press, 1980); C.E. Welch (ed.), *Civilian Control of the Military* (Albany: State University of New York Press, 1976).

10. The data sources are identical to those outlined above in note 7. In contrast to most of our variables the domestic conflict variables are not lagged by a year.

11. The mean values for percentage of executive posts held by the military are: 9.8 (1954), 14.2 (1958), 8.7 (1962), 10.5 (1966), 14.1 (1970), 14.5 (1974), 19.2 (1978), 13.2 (1982). The average percentage moves from 10.8 to 15.3 from the first to the second set of four test years.

12. With the slight exception of 1954, the correlations between percentage of executive posts held by the military and a dummy for presence of a military regime are both significant and high. The correlations are: 0.30 (1954), 0.68 (1958), 0.71 (1962), 0.76 (1966), 0.68 (1970), 0.70 (1974), 0.74 (1978), 0.66 (1982).

13. Regressions of military expenditure on GDP and a dummy for presence of a military regime do not produce a significant coefficient for the dummy in any year.

14. We have already noted that percentage of cabinet posts held by the military is strangely distributed (primarily because higher values are associated with military regimes). Furthermore, it is somewhat arbitrary as to at what level, say 10 per cent or 30 per cent or 50 per cent, we might regard the percentage of posts held by the military to be critical. Consequently, we try several permutations of the percentage executive posts variable. We use it in its raw form as an interval variable, we use it categorized as a dummy (above and below 10 per cent) and we use it as a two-stage dummy (0–33 per cent, 34–67 per cent, and 67–100 per cent). Controlling for GDP, we find none of these measures produces a significant equation.

15. There are no significant negative correlations between levels of relative military expenditure and the occurrence of a coup. In fact there are no significant correlations at all, which in turn means coups are not more likely in countries already sensitized to a high level of military commitment. There are also incidentally no significant correlations between occurrence of coups and percentage military in the executive, which in turn means that the military does not use any increased exposure to governmental office to encourage it to make a coup.

16. As a final note to this section we confront a final objection to our arguments. It could be argued that an effect on military expenditure from direct military influence would require a sustained period of influence. We test for this by accumulating number of years of military regime and percentage of executive posts held by the military over a four-year period prior to the test year. Regressing military expenditure on these variables we find, controlling for GDP, only two significant effects. In 1954 percentage of executive posts is a negative predictor, while in 1966 accumulated military regime is a positive predictor. Since we find only one effect in the hypothesized direction (and that, though significant, has a small beta value) we conclude that neither direct influence nor sustained direct influence predicts to military expenditure.

17. Averaged over the second as opposed to the first set of four test years, the relative incidence of domestic conflict increases 1.4 times. The increase is more marked for organized as compared with unorganized (1.5 times as against 1.2 times) and for sustained as compared with sporadic (1.6 times as against 1.2 times).

18. In only two of our test years do we get a significant equation for the regression of relative military expenditure on the dummy for domestic conflict (1954 and 1966).

19. We regress relative military expenditure on three separate equations, each containing two dummy variables. Thus, relative military is regressed on a dummy measuring presence of unorganized and a dummy measuring presence of organized conflict. The constant term is the mean value for those cases having no conflict, while the mean values for those countries, respectively experiencing unorganized and organized conflict, are given by their b coefficients plus the constant. The significance level of each b coefficient is in effect a difference of means test between that category and the category of countries having no conflict. The b coefficients for unorganized and sporadic conflict are never significant. The b coefficients are significant for organized and sustained conflict, respectively, in the test years 1966, 1970 and 1962, 1966, 1970. Concerning regionalized and generalized conflict, we had expected generalized to be the better measure of a high level of conflict. In fact generalized conflict never produces a significant b coefficient, while regionalized does so only in one test year (1966). We infer that geographic location, contrary to our expectations, is not a sensitive measure of the intensity of conflict.

20. For the combined effect we use a dummy measuring joint occurrence of both organized and sustained conflict and obtain significant results in four test years (1962, 1966, 1970, 1978). To test for an interaction effect (i.e. whether the occurrence of both organized and sustained conflict raises military expenditure more than just a summed effect), we use three dummies of: presence of organized, presence of sustained, and presence of both organized and sustained conflict. The interactive equations do not yield significant results.

21. It seems entirely plausible that the military may constitute part of the object against which any group may protest. Indeed it seems particularly likely, at higher levels of conflict, that the military may be an explicit object of protest in that it is likely to be

associated with the government. In this respect then the military can constitute a source of conflict. There seems to us, however, no reason to anticipate any relation between military expenditure and the military as a source of conflict.

22. We have then significant equations in five of eight test years (the exceptions being 1958, 1974, and 1982). The mean R^2 value for the significant equations is 0.13.

23. The b coefficients, since we use dummies, give a direct measure, in their anti-logged form, of the proportionate increase in military expenditure brought about by the presence of the dummy. Generally speaking, sustained conflict has a slightly greater impact than organized. The average increase across the five significant test years for the proportionate increase in relative military expenditure is 2.4.

7 Military Expenditure and Interstate Conflict

Introduction

This chapter continues the preoccupation with conflict but switches the focus from a domestic to the interstate level. Interstate conflict can be perpetrated through a variety of means, such as propaganda, diplomacy, economic pressure, or subversion. Our focus centres purely on conflict carried out through armed forces. Consequently for the purposes of this chapter interstate conflict is synonymous with conflict pursued through the employment of organized force or, in other words, with war.

Our general working hypothesis is that, other things being equal, interstate conflict predicts positively to military expenditure. As such we postulate that military expenditure, in part, is a response to interstate conflict. This leads us to expect, firstly, that military expenditure will rise and fall around interstate conflict and, secondly that military expenditure will be sensitive to the different levels of intensity of interstate conflict.

Before elaborating the rationale that underpins our general working hypothesis, we should emphasize that we do not even begin to confront the issue area of the substantive causes of war. The subject of war, eminently understandably, has attracted considerable attention and indeed has spawned some truly monumental studies.[1] Insightful and interesting though this research has been, it has most assuredly not produced any agreed or coherent theory of interstate conflict.[2]

Although we do not wish to become deeply involved in the debate on the causes of war, primarily because we could not conceivably contribute anything of any value, we do need, for the establishment of our rationale, to make some incursions into this literature.

There are a variety of approaches which seem to us to have some limitations. For example, some approach war from a purely system-level perspective, attributing war to such diverse general conditions as capitalism or imperialism or international anarchy. These conditions, quite apart from being rather vague, are enduring. Since war is highly irregular and decidedly uncommon, there seems to us to be something of a misfit. Another approach is to explain war in terms of the object of contention of the conflict, which results in a classification of war in terms of conflicting political or economic or religious or ideological interests and so on. Such a classification not only becomes extremely long very quickly but seems to be much more of a typology than an explanation. Furthermore, it begs the question of why, for instance, conflicting political interests on only relatively few occasions result in war.

A potentially more profitable approach begins by asking whether war is a unique or autonomous phenomenon or whether it is a manifestation of a more general and ubiquitous process. Many approaches, particularly to interstate war, seem to us to follow, as in the examples above, the former position. A more profitable and nomothetic approach is to view war as a manifestation of the use of force and to begin a more generalized and abstract explanation by asking what explains the use of force. Our view, in keeping in part with numerous other writers, is that the use of force is not a manifestation of some pathological deviation but is explained in terms of its utility. The primary utility of force is that it provides the possibility of pursuing an interest, which is to be promoted or protected, when other means of pursuing that interest, such as persuasion or negotiation or non-forceful coercion, are perceived to be less efficient or potentially unsuccessful. Two or more parties, therefore, may rationally engage in forceful conflict when they decide they can gain more through deploying force than not so doing. Decisions to employ force are first and foremost then a product of a comparative calculation of the rewards and costs accruing to the variety of different means of promoting or protecting some interest.

Our objective, thus far, has explicitly not been to produce an explanation of war but rather to specify in an admittedly abstract and brief form how we conceptualize war. We see it, in sum, as a subset of a much larger set of events, namely conflict pursued through coercion, which occurs whenever two or more parties conclude on the basis of a comparative evaluation of rewards and costs across a range of different means of pursuing interests that force holds the promise of the highest net reward or lowest net cost.

We have pursued this discussion purely to amplify the two critical components of our general working hypothesis, namely that military expenditure is a response to interstate conflict and that the response is one which stimulates expenditure.

Considering first the relationship of conflict to military expenditure, we consider that the latter is a response to the former, rather vice versa, on three main grounds. First, we do not consider the military, let alone levels of military expenditure to constitute one of the core substantive interests to be promoted or protected through the deployment of force. While states can and do decide to go to war on the basis of a host of substantive interests, we do not consider military expenditure to be one of these. Second, the utility of force is not created by the military but exists quite independently of the military. Far from providing an explanation or rationale of force, the military rather constitutes simply the means whereby force, in one particular setting, namely the international system, is manifested. Third, the decision to employ force is only very tangentially connected to military expenditure. Such a decision we take to be a function of the comparative evaluation of net rewards accruing across a variety of different means of pursuing interests. The rewards and costs accruing to the use of military force are initially, therefore, only a part of a much larger calculus. Furthermore, though some calculation based on military expenditure can be incorporated into reward and cost evaluations of the use of force, many such rewards and costs are relatively constant and enduring and, as such, independent of levels of expenditure. Moreover, it is not so much any state's level of expenditure but ratios of expenditure across states that would be critical.

If military expenditure does not drive war, a subject to which we return below in discussing our results, then we must be able to answer the question of why should conflict drive up levels of military expenditure. In one critical respect this relationship undoubtedly seems bizarre. If we assume, as seems perfectly reasonable, that the outcome of a conflict is strongly related, other things being equal, to the ratio of capabilities between, say, two states, then the outcome would be the same irrespective of whether the conflict is conducted with military expenditure equal to 1 per cent or 10 per cent of GDP. In other words, if two states have decided they can gain more or lose less by engaging in war, why should they raise their military commitments when the outcome would be the same at a lower and therefore less expensive level?

Several factors, we suggest, could be responsible for this apparently bizarre behaviour. First, in committing themselves either voluntarily or involuntarily to armed conflict, states immediately begin to use a means of promoting interests which normally is not directly employed. In this respect, therefore, conflict automatically entails some special priority to military capabilities. Second, it seems somewhat unrealistic, albeit entirely rational, that states should agree to conduct a conflict at a frozen pre-conflict level of military expenditure. If they could display such a degree of co-operation, it is highly unlikely they would have a conflict in the first place. Third, there are some good reasons to think of military conflict in zero-sum terms. Though it is unquestionably the case that military and political victories are not synonymous, this is unlikely to figure prominently certainly as states decide to engage in war. Since military victory, presumably at least the primary objective, approximates at the extreme to a zero-sum situation, then it seems eminently likely that states would take appropriate action to ensure that they do not incur defeat. Such an appropriate action would well seem to be an expansion of military capabilities. Finally, it seems very plausible that some degree of mutual misperception would take place. For example, one side may well conclude that it may achieve an advantage over the other if it increased its capabilities. Since the other side is likely to make precisely the same calculation, then we would find a mutual increase. Or again, each side may independently come to the conclusion that the conflict would be faster if it were pursued more intensely. Once more, then, mutual misperception, namely the inability to realize the other side may make identical calculations, would result in mutual increase of expenditure.

In sum, we conceptualize war as that condition in which a constellation of factors, unknown to us and in effect then taken as a given, leads two or more states to have recourse to the use of force. Such a recourse we assume takes place because the states in question have mutually concluded that by employing force the net rewards will be greater or the net costs will be lower than by pursuing any of a variety of other forms of interest promotion or protection. Due either to the priority now attached to military capabilities or to the inability through co-operative breakdown to freeze levels of expenditure or to the zero-sum of military victory or to mutual misperception, we hypothesize therefore that armed conflict will stimulate military expenditure.

We turn now to outline the measurement of the variable of interstate conflict. Such conflict we take to be present when the troops of any two or more countries come into armed conflict. It is categorized into four levels that we take to be ordinal. The first entails small-scale contact entailing only very partial mobilization, such as border skirmishes or very temporary and limited invasions. The second level is defined by a state deploying its military outside its own borders in the internal conflict of another state. The employment of troops must, however, explicitly fall short of a full commitment. The third level is characterized when a state confronts within its own territory foreign troops deployed in its own internal conflict explicitly against it. The foreign troops must explicitly not represent a full commitment. The final level represents mutual, full and direct commitment of troops on the part of two or more states. The location of the conflict and the presence or absence of domestic conflict are immaterial.[3]

Findings

On a purely descriptive level, though interstate conflict is not as widespread as domestic conflict, it is nonetheless relatively pronounced. As measured by us, some 56 per cent of our population of Third World countries manifest some form of interstate conflict as opposed to some 84 per cent that experience some form of domestic conflict. Further, as we see from Table 7.1, while there is no indication of any sustained increase in the incidence of interstate conflict, there is equally no sign of any decrease. Though interstate conflict in general may not be increasing, it is, however, the case that it is more likely over time to take a more intense form.

Table 7.1: Percentage frequencies of Third World countries experiencing interstate conflict by level of conflict, selected years 1950–4 to 1978–82

Year	Level of interstate conflict					
	0	1	2	3	4	(N)
1950–54	78	17	0	6	0	18
1954–58	52	37	4	7	0	27
1958–62	63	35	0	2	0	43
1962–66	73	17	2	2	6	64
1966–70	72	11	5	3	9	79
1970–74	72	10	10	1	7	81
1974–78	61	19	9	4	8	79
1978–82	60	22	10	0	8	60

Thus, comparing the first set of four test years with the second we see that, while the incidence of interstate conflict scarcely changes, the propensity of states to engage in interstate conflict beyond the level of border skirmishes increases two and a half times.[4]

Our interest centres of course not so much on descriptive characteristics of interstate conflict but rather on its impact on military expenditure. In general, we find that interstate conflict has a very powerful stimulative effect on military expenditure, a result which we now elaborate through several stages.

The first step of the first stage is to examine quite simply whether interstate conflict, represented as a dummy or categoric variable, has an influence on military expenditure (see Table 7.2). Amalgamating all levels of interstate

Table 7.2: Regression results for relative military expenditure on dummy for interstate conflict and for dummies for levels of interstate conflict, selected years 1954–82

Year	Dummy interstate conflict (DI) coefficients	R^2	Dummies for levels of interstate conflict (1–4) coefficients		R^2
1954	0.23 + 0.45 (DI)	0.32	0.23 + 0.36 (1) + 0.41	0.72 (4) 0.44	0.33
1958	0.32 + 0.34 (DI)	0.18	0.32 + 0.34 (1)		0.18
1962	NS		NS		
1966	0.23 + 0.50 (DI)	0.29	0.23 + 0.51 (1) + (0.44)	0.37 (2) (0.12)*	
			+ 0.37 (3) + (0.12)*	0.57 (4) (0.32)	0.29
1970	0.32 + 0.45 (DI)	0.18	0.32 + 0.60 (1) + (0.42)	0.35 (2) (0.16)*	
			+ 0.78 (3) + (0.21)	0.12 (4) (0.05)*	0.23
1974	0.25 + 0.62 (DI)	0.39	0.25 + 0.32 (1)+ (0.20)	0.59 (2) (0.37)	
			+ 1.08 (3) + (0.24)	1.00 (4) (0.58)	0.52
1978	0.41 + 0.31 (DI)	0.10	0.41 + 0.07 (1) + (0.05)*	0.58 (2) (0.31)	
			+ 0.35 (3) + (0.09)*	0.53 (4) (0.28)	0.17
1982	0.41 + 0.28 (DI)	0.10	0.41 + 0.16 (1)+ (0.15)*	0.47 (2) (0.39)	
			+ 0.11 (4) (0.03)*		0.15

*Not significant at 0.05 level or higher.

conflict into a simple measure of presence of interstate conflict, we find that re-gressions of relative military expenditure on this dummy yield significant and positive results in all but one test years. If it is the case furthermore that it is not just simply that interstate conflict predicts to military expenditure but that higher levels of conflict predict to higher levels of military expenditure, then we would expect regressions of relative military expenditure on a set of dummy or categoric variables profiling different levels of conflict to produce equations with higher R^2 values and b coefficients that increase across the different levels. Though there are some complications with this procedure, due to the small number of cases for some levels of conflict in some years, this expectation is generally met.[5]

Although interstate conflict is measured, correctly in our view, as a discrete variable, it is conceivable that there are elements of continuity associated with it, which could be weakening our results. In particular, it is possible that there could be what we might call a continuation effect. We already know that interstate conflict is significantly associated with higher levels of expenditure and it seems plausible that such levels may remain high even after hostilities have ceased either because some tension may continue or because of bureaucratic pressure on the part of the military that resists a reduction in expenditure. Of these two possible explanations of a continuation effect we do in fact favour the former, given the results of the last chapter. If there were to be a continuation effect, then amalgamating any manifestations of interstate conflict over a number of years up to and including the year of measurement of military expenditure would provide more powerful results than these noted in Table 7.2.[6]

Consequently, we construct a new set of dummy variables based on the presence of interstate conflict in any of the five years up to and including the year of measurement of military expenditure and repeat the above analysis. Generally speaking, as we see from Table 7.3, the expectation that this will produce stronger equations is met. The improvement in the equations does signify that there is a continuation effect, though it is not actually as pronounced as we had anticipated. We return to this in more detail below.[7]

As a final elaboration of this stage we investigate different combinations of the various levels of interstate violence. The principal motivation for this is that we are having some difficulties using, including absence of conflict, five levels of conflict with insufficient numbers of cases at all these levels. Both conceptually and statistically the most pleasing outcome is to think in terms of three levels: none, low and high conflict corresponding respectively to no interstate conflict, border skirmish (the previous level 1) and all other higher forms of conflict (pre-viously levels 2 through 4). This is the categorization with which we operate henceforth and Table 7.4 produces our main results of this first stage of investi-gation.[9]

At the conclusion of the first stage we may note four principal results. First, interstate conflict generally speaking has a pronounced stimulative impact on military expenditure. Interpreting our b coefficients, interstate conflict has the effect, other things being equal, of almost doubling to trebling relative military expenditure. Second, the impact of interstate conflict varies systematically for the

Table 7.3: Regression results for relative military expenditure on dummy for interstate conflict and dummies for levels of interstate conflict, selected years 1950–54 to 1978–82

Year	Dummy interstate conflict (DI) coefficients	R^2	Dummies for levels of interstate conflict (1–4) coefficients	R^2
1950–4	NS		0.21 + 0.35(1) − 0.33(3) (0.51) (−0.23)*	0.33
1954–58	NS		0.32 + 0.27(1) + 0.50(2) (0.41) (0.27)* − 0.20(3) (−0.15)*	0.26
1958–62	0.29 + 0.22(DI)	0.09	NS	
1962–66	0.22 + 0.47(DI)	0.34	0.22 + 0.47(1) + 0.38(2) (0.51) (0.13)* + 0.38(3) + 0.48(4) (0.13)* (0.33)	0.34
1966–70	0.25 + 0.44(DI)	0.26	0.25 + 0.37(1) + 0.33(2) (0.31) (0.18)* + 0.31(3) + 0.64(4) (0.12)* (0.46)	0.29
1970–74	0.25 + 0.52(DI)	0.35	0.25 + 0.21(1) + 0.51(2) (0.16)* (0.39) + 1.06(3) + 0.85(4) (0.30) (0.57)	0.49
1974–78	0.32 + 0.39(DI)	0.22	0.32 + 0.18(1) + 0.71(2) (0.17)* (0.49) + 0.68(3) + 0.41(4) (0.32) (0.29)	0.35
1978–82	0.37 + 0.28(DI)	0.13	0.37 + 0.19(1) + 0.36(2) (0.20)* (0.29) + 0.45(4) (0.36)	0.18

*Not significant at 0.05 level or above.

most part with the level of conflict. Low conflict on average, other things being equal, doubles relative military expenditure, while high conflict, on average, trebles it. Interstate conflict, in other words is associated with increases of very substantial proportions in military expenditure. Third, though we investigate this in more detail below, there does appear to be a continuation effect from interstate conflict. In other words, there is something of a propensity for military expenditure to remain higher even after actual hostilities have ceased. Finally, there is a tendency for the influence of low conflict to become less marked over time. Though we are not entirely sure of the reason for this, we have some confidence in the following argument. Countries that have experienced interstate conflict

Table 7.4: Regression results for relative military expenditure
on dummy for interstate conflict and dummies for low and high levels
of interstate conflict, selected years 1950–54 to 1978–82

Year	Dummy interstate conflict (DI) coefficients	R^2	Dummies for low (L) and high (H) levels of interstate conflict coefficients			R^2
1950–54	NS		0.21 +	0.35 (L) – (0.51)	0.33 (H) (–0.23)*	0.33
1954–58	NS			NS		
1958–62	0.26 + 0.25 (DI)	0.13	0.26 +	0.25 (L) + (0.37)	0.20 H (0.09)*	0.14
1962–66	0.17 + 0.51 (DI)	0.46	0.17 +	0.52 (L) + (0.59)	0.49 (H) (0.44)	0.46
1966–70	0.23 + 0.47 (DI)	0.32	0.23 +	0.46 (L) + (0.35)	0.52 (H) (0.51)	0.32
1970–74	0.25 + 0.52 (DI)	0.35	0.25 +	0.21 (L) + (0.16)*	0.68 (H) (0.67)	0.45
1974–78	0.28 + 0.43 (DI)	0.29	0.28 +	0.21 (L)+ (0.22)	0.63 (H) (0.65)	0.40
1978–82	0.35 + 0.31 (DI)	0.16	0.35 +	0.20 (L) + (0.22)*	0.44 (H) (0.45)	0.20

*Not significant at 0.05 level or above.

and thereby higher levels of military expenditure though reducing their expenditure after the conflict nonetheless may have higher levels of expenditure than countries that have never experienced interstate conflict. Thus, on returning to the no-conflict category they bid up the mean and dispersion within this category, thereby making it more difficult to find a significant difference between the no- and low-conflict categories.[9]

The second stage of our investigation of interstate conflict entails an examination of the duration of conflict. This in effect provides us with a second dimension of conflict intensity to complement that which has already been introduced through the levels measure. Thus, other things being equal, we would again hypothesize that the more intense the conflict, intensity now being synonymous with duration, the higher the level of military expenditure.

Duration of interstate conflict is measured in two forms: by simply aggregating total number of years to form an interval variable ranging for each test period from zero to five, and by profiling years in terms of a set of dummies.[10]

Regressions of relative military expenditure on years of conflict yield results, as may be seen from Table 7.5, that corroborate the hypothesis that the greater the duration of conflict the higher the level of military expenditure.[11] We see furthermore from the two sets of results that there are no grounds for supposing that

Table 7.5: Regression results for relative military expenditure on duration of interstate conflict as measured both in continuous and dummy form, selected years 1950–4 to 1978–82

Year	Duration in continuous form (Y) Coefficients	R^2	Duration as set of dummies (1–5) Coefficients		R^2
1950–54	NS		NS		
1954–58	0.32 + 0.08 (Y)	0.20	NS		
1958–62	0.28 + 0.09 (Y)	0.16	NS		
1962–66	0.19 + 0.15 (Y)	0.46	0.17 + 0.37 (1) + (0.27)	0.52 (2) (0.33)	
			+ 0.45 (3) + (0.29)	0.45 (4) (0.33)	
			+ 0.83 (5) (0.53)		0.52
1966–70	0.24 + 0.17 (Y)	0.44	0.23 + 0.25 (1) + (0.23)	0.50 (2) (0.21)	
			+ 0.58 (3) + (0.24)	0.28 (4) (0.08)*	
			+ 0.88 (5) (0.62)		0.46
1970–74	0.28 + 0.18 (Y)	0.37	0.25 + 0.33 (1) + (0.24)	0.44 (2) (0.21)	
			+ 0.64 (3) + (0.51)	0.51 (4) (0.20)	
			+ 0.78 (5) (0.31)		0.40
1974–78	0.31 + 0.15 (Y)	0.29	0.28 + 0.28 (1) + (0.26)	0.43 (2) (0.33)	
			+ 0.66 (3) + (0.42)	0.42 (4) (0.21)	
			+ 0.64 (5) (0.32)		0.34
1978–82	0.36 + 0.12 (Y)	0.24	0.35 + 0.15 (1) + (0.14)*	0.37 (2) (0.27)	
			− 0.06 (3) + (−0.03)*	0.42 (4) (0.24)	
			+ 0.64 (5) (0.47)		0.29

*Not significant at 0.05 level or above.

Table 7.6: Regression results for relative military expenditure on dummies profiling combinations of levels and duration of interstate conflict, selected years 1950–54 to 1978–82

Year	Coefficients				R^2
1950–54	NS				
1954–58	NS				
1958–62	0.26 +	0.17 (12–) + (0.22)*	0.42 (13+) + (0.41)	0.20 (22–) (0.09)	0.18
1962–66	0.17 +	0.47 (12–) + (0.39)	0.56 (13+) + (0.49)	0.33 (22–) (0.18)*	
		+ 0.57 (23+) (0.42)			0.48
1966–70	0.23 +	0.40 (12–) + (0.32)	0.48 (13+) + (0.14)*	0.10 (22–) (0.07)*	
		+ 0.78 (23+) (0.62)			0.45
1970–74	0.25 +	0.16 (12–) + (0.10)*	0.29 (13+) + (0.14)*	0.56 (22–) (0.34)	
		+ 0.75 (23+) (0.62)			0.46
1974–78	0.28 +	0.15 (12–) + (0.13)*	0.38 (13+) + (0.22)*	0.57 (22–) (0.47)	
		+ 0.71 (23+) (0.52)			0.42
1978–82	0.35 +	0.25 (12–) – (0.26)	0.06 (13+) + (–0.03)*	0.13 (22–) (0.08)*	
		+ 0.56 (23+) (0.50)			0.27

*Not significant at the 0.05 level or above.

duration behaves in a non-linear manner.[12]

Generally speaking the regressions employing duration and levels of conflict produce broadly similar results. In effect we learn much the same about military expenditure, irrespective of whether we explain it in terms of intensity as measured by duration or intensity as measured by level. The next evident step of course is to investigate whether we improve our level of explanation employing both measures.

This step raises a slightly awkward problem in that while there is no *a priori* reason to suppose that low-level conflicts would be of any greater or shorter duration than high-level ones, there must of necessity be a positive correlation between duration and levels of conflict. In other words, duration and levels are not independent. the most appropriate solution to this difficulty is to combine duration and level into single variables.[13]

In the regression results presented in Table 7.6 we look for two things. First, if both measures of intensity combined augmented an explanation of levels of military expenditure, then we should expect to find higher R^2 values than in the equations above. Second, we may look for the relative importance of each measure of intensity. If level of conflict prevailed over duration, then the b coefficients for high conflict would be higher than those for low conflict irrespective of duration. Conversely if duration prevailed over level, then the b coefficients for longer duration would be higher than those for shorter duration, irrespective of level of conflict. If there were both effects, then the b coefficients would progressively increase as we moved from shorter duration low-level conflict through to longer duration high-level conflict.

The results in Table 7.6 are not as powerful as we might have hoped and they are, at least initially, slightly complex, a complexity that includes one or two undesired results.[14] Nonetheless, three relatively clear and strong conclusions may be drawn. First, taking into account both measures of intensity does improve our explanation of military expenditure levels, though the improvement is not nearly as marked as we would have liked. Second, there is, generally speaking, evidence of both effects. Thus, holding constant duration, level increases military expenditure, and vice versa. Third, the main complexity of the results of Table 7.6, which is rather interesting, is that there is an interaction effect. Thus, duration tends to increase military expenditure differentially in the two levels of conflict such that longer duration in the high-level category produces higher levels of military expenditure than we would expect on the basis of a simple additive result.[15]

In sum, intensity of interstate conflict, as measured by duration, does influence positively levels of military expenditure. Though we cannot escape the result that duration and intensity both have very similar aggregate influences and both have independent effects, our preferred evaluation is to attach some priority to levels of conflict. This is not based principally on statistical criteria (indeed the results do not permit such a clear decision to be made) but on the grounds that the differentiations between no conflict, border skirmishes, and higher levels seem to us to represent clear qualitative steps, which are 'theoretically' more interesting than simple duration. Consequently, we view levels of conflict as the more important determinant, seeing then duration as being a further determinant, which positively qualifies level in an interactive manner, increasing military expenditure more in the high than the low-conflict category.

Our third stage of the analysis of the impact of interstate conflict is analogous to the second in that it takes the basic results of the first stage, where we would argue we have established the existence of a powerful conflict effect, and attempts to refine them. The focus of this stage is on what we choose to call a decay effect. Decay is measured in terms of the distance in time of the cessation of the conflict from the year of measurement of military expenditure. In this context, then, we hypothesize that the greater the decay, given an increase in military expenditure contingent on the occurrence of interstate conflict, the lower the level of military expenditure. Our interest in decay is twofold. First, we have already argued above for a continuation effect in justifying the measurement of interstate conflict across five years. The examination of decay, in effect the obverse of continuation, permits a more refined elaboration of the importance of the influence of continuation. Second, one difficulty with the analysis of the impact of duration is that we have not taken account of when the conflict occurred but only for how long it endures.[16]

Decay, like duration, is measured both as a continuous variable and as a set of dummies.[17] The findings from each type of measurement yield broadly similar results, indicating that there is indeed a significant decay effect. In other words, the level of military expenditure is lower as the cessation of hostilities becomes more distant in time.[18] As in the case of our analysis of duration, we then proceed to construct a set of independent variables, combining level of conflict and degree of decay. Since the time frame of decay is so important we run this analysis over both five- and nine-year time-spans.[19]

Table 7.7: Regression results for relative military expenditure on dummies profiling combinations of levels and decay of interstate conflict, selected years 1950–4 to 1978–82

Year	Coefficients	R^2
1950–54	NS	
1954–58	NS	
1958–62	NS	
1962–66	0.17 − 0.13 (12−) + 0.58 (13+) + 0.49 (23+) (−0.05)* (0.64) (0.44)	0.53
1966–70	0.23 + 0.39 (12−) + 0.44 (13+) + 0.29 (22−) (0.25) (0.26) (0.15)* + 0.58 (23+) (0.52)	0.34
1970–74	0.25 + 0.21 (13+) + 0.22 (22−) + 0.72 (23+) (0.16)* (0.06)* (0.69)	0.46
1974–78	0.28 + 0.40 (12−) + 0.18 (13+) + 1.01 (22−) (0.16)* (0.18) (0.41) + 0.57 (23+) (0.57)	0.44
1978–82	0.35 + 0.25 (12+) − 0.19 (13+) + 0.46 (22−) (0.14)* (00.19)* (0.16)* + 0.44 (23+) (0.43)	0.20

*Not significant at the 0.05 level or beyond.

Table 7.8: Regression results for relative military expenditure on dummies profiling combinations of levels and decay of interstate conflict, selected years 1958–66 to 1974–82

Year	Coefficients			R^2
1958–66	0.19 − 0.06 (1D1) − (−0.05)* + 0.44 (2D3) (0.45)	0.07 (1D2) + (−0.04)*	0.64 (1D3) (0.66)	0.55
1962–70	0.22 − 0.04 (1D1) + (−0.01)* + 0.15 (2D1 + (0.05)*	0.38 (1D2) + (0.21) 0.55 (2D2) + (0.36)	0.59 (1D3) (0.33) 0.60 (2D3) (0.57)	0.47
1966–74	0.22 + 0.36 (1D1) + (0.15)* + 0.06 (2D1) + (0.02)*	0.43 (1D2) + (0.21) 0.09 (2D2) + (0.04)*	0.20 (1D3) (0.15)* 0.73 (2D3) (0.71)	0.50
1970–78	0.26 + 0.16 (1D1) + (0.13)* + 0.67 (2D2) + (0.56)	0.38 (1D2) + (0.16)* 0.65 (2D3) (0.41)	0.47 (2D1) (0.35)	0.46
1974–82	0.32 + 0.23 (1D1)+ (0.11)* − 0.04 (2D1) + (−0.01)*	0.28 (1D2) + (0.18)* 0.50 (2D2) + (0.24)	0.06 (1D3) (0.05)* 0.54 (2D3) (0.57)	0.34

*Not significant at the 0.05 level or beyond.

The results contained in Tables 7.7 and 7.8 are not as clear or tidy as we may have wished, in the sense that coefficients within either level of conflict do not always increase linearly in a consistent manner. Nonetheless, the result are sufficiently strong to show clear evidence of decay. Furthermore, decay tends to be more rapid in the low conflict category. In the high-conflict category decay does not really begin to appear until some 3–6 years after the conflict and even over this period it is less, rather than more, likely to be marked. However, 6–9 years after the conflict, decay is very pronounced. Indeed, after six years it is impossible on average to distinguish, in terms of levels of military expenditure, those countries that have experienced high levels of conflict from those that have not.[20]

The absence of entirely consistent results we take to be a function of two main factors. In the first place, there is an expected partial lack of clarity because the cessation of conflict, the initiation of which brings a sharp increase in military spending, stimulates two opposing tendencies in the form of continuation and decay effects. In other words, the continuation effect is not as pronounced as it might be precisely because it is undermined to some degree by a decay effect, which concomitantly is not as pronounced as it might be because it too is undermined by a continuation effect.

The second main reason contributing to some lack of consistency in direction of the coefficients pertains we suspect to problems of aggregation. Some countries are more inclined than others to reduce more rapidly their military expenditure after the termination of conflict.[12] Other things being equal, we might expect this to balance across countries. However, we deal in general with a sufficiently small number of countries, which differs over time, that we suspect that a balance is not equally achieved in every test year. In other words, some test years will for instance contain a greater proportion of countries that show, say, more rapid decay, which would produce the type of inconsistency that we see in our results.[22]

Though it is important to note these problems, they should not detract from our main finding that there is indeed a marked propensity for military expenditure to decay after the termination of interstate conflict. This decay, particularly for those countries that have experienced high levels of conflict, is however far from instantaneous but is in fact postponed by a continuation effect. Nonetheless, decay does finally prevail over continuation such that on average around six years after the termination of conflict it is impossible to distinguish at least by military expenditure levels those countries that have and have not experienced conflict, irrespective of the level of conflict.

Before turning to the fourth and final stage of our examination of interstate conflict, we consider three sets of criticisms that may be levelled against our analysis.

The first would accept, as we posit, that levels of military expenditure are indeed in part a response to interstate conflict but argue that the relationship of conflict to military expenditure is an uninteresting or spurious one. This could be argued firstly by suggesting that the military has an interest in justifying its existence, which it can do by engaging in war. Since war entails higher expenditure we therefore find exactly the relationship we have noted above. It would then not be war but rather a military preoccupation with self-justification that would be responsible for the higher levels of expenditure. A second variant would be that interstate conflict, which entails higher levels of expenditure, is simply a vehicle for the military to promote its own interests. Again war would be a spurious variable and the real predictor would be the promotion by the military of its own interests. We find both variants unacceptable. The military can have recourse to numerous justifications for its existence without having recourse to war. Furthermore, since the majority of countries do not go to war, and even those that do will do so irregularly, then presumably many militaries would be left without any justification. As regards the second variant, if the military does not increase its expenditure in any systematic manner in the situation of military regimes, it would seem extremely circuitous that it would have recourse to a more difficult route, that of war, so to do.

A second and decidedly more complex criticism would be that we have wrongly ordered our dependent and independent variables. Rather than hypothesizing that higher levels of military expenditure are a response to interstate conflict, we should rather be hypothesizing that interstate conflict is a result of military expenditure. The rationale, explaining a predicted relationship from military expenditure to conflict, would stipulate that higher levels of military expenditure in effect sensitize countries to a greater readiness to use conflict as a means of promoting their interests or resolving disputes. While we have some sympathy, as will become clear in the conclusion, with a not too distant variant of this rationale, we do not accept for two main reasons that military expenditure predicts strongly to conflict.

In the first place it would give rise to a strange automation type of explanation of conflict, which incorporated a staggering degree of precision. While there is no accepted theory of war, research on war, to the best of our knowledge, understandably emphasizes substantive clashes of interest as the most immediate explanatory factors. Wars are a product of competing and usually incompatible sets of economic or political or socio-cultural claims rather than levels of military expenditure.[23] Though it may be true that interstate conflict presupposes national militaries, this is really nothing more than a tautology in which the significance of the military is as a means or vehicle for the conduct of conflict rather than as a root cause. The divorcing of an explanation of conflict from competing substantive goals or interests and ascribing conflict to levels of military expenditure implies a rather strange automation view of war. There is furthermore within this automation view what appears to us as a highly unrealistic degree of precision. Thus, when military expenditure rises to a particular level border skirmishes would ensue. As it rises to yet a higher level still, then border skirmishes would be transformed to full-scale war.[24] It seems decidedly more likely to us to suggest that different sets of conflicts of interest underlie these two different forms of conflict and that since the latter requires a much more substantial commitment of resources than the former it consequently produces higher levels of military expenditure.

Our second reservation is that a relationship predicting from military expenditure to war does not fit across the whole range of our findings. If we took the results from any one test year, in which relative military expenditure is significantly related to conflict, then it might be thought that this would corroborate a military expenditure to conflict relationship, as this later hypothesis is quite consistent with the finding that states at war would have higher levels of military expenditure. However, this hypothesis would also postulate that there exists a substantial number of countries which have higher levels of military expenditure but are not actually at war but about to go to war some time in the near future. This has to be the case since we know that war is not an enduring condition. Such states would be classified in the no conflict category. We would therefore expect that the no-conflict category would not only show substantially greater variation than the conflict category, which is not the case, but also it would be extremely difficult to find a significant relationship between military expenditure and conflict, which again is consistently not the case.

Furthermore, while we can provide straightforward interpretations to our findings on duration and decay, the hypothesis of military expenditure to conflict either could only give in our view convoluted explanations or would suggest that we should not be getting the results we do. As an example of the former it is difficult to understand why expenditure should show a marked propensity to decline after a conflict.[25] As an example of the latter, consistently the easiest category to identify in terms of levels of military expenditure is that group which is currently experiencing or has just experienced a major conflict. On par with this category, according to the military expenditure to conflict thesis, would be all those states about to go to war. If such a category did exist we would be unable to find the distinctive group produced in our results. Not only does the hypothesis predicting from military expenditure to conflict not readily fit results outlined immediately above but it also does not accord with other of our results. Thus, this opposing hypothesis would imply to us that we would be looking in effect to a two-tiered or bipolar distribution of military expenditure in which the upper tier profiled enduringly high levels and was much more conflict-prone. There is no evidence of a bipolar distribution. Furthermore, while some states do endure at relatively high levels of expenditure, the high expenditure countries are far from being entirely stable. Finally, countries that do persist at higher levels are not, as we see in more detail later, significantly more conflict-prone.

In sum we do not accept the military expenditure to conflict thesis. An interpretation of what we take to be a rather extensive set of results whereby military expenditure is seen as a response to conflict seems to us decidedly more robust.

The third and final criticism of our results and interpretation, which is at least in part related to the point above, is that we have not sufficiently well established a causal link from conflict to levels of military expenditure. Though it is certainly not essential for our purposes to demonstrate that all high levels of military expenditure are a function of interstate-state conflict, it is essential if high levels of military expenditure are to be seen at least in part as a response to conflict that we do need evidence of military expenditure rising and falling around any such conflict.

We have already in our findings on decay produced some rather impressive evidence of expenditure falling subsequent to conflict. In order that expenditure can fall it must in the first place rise, in which respect we might reasonably expect that the conflict raised it. It is, however, conceivable that something other than the conflict was responsible for the rise. Though we would in principle think this unlikely, it is the case that cross-sectional analysis can produce misleading results, though it is rare that this would happen in repeated cross-sectional tests.[26] Since these findings are, however, of sufficient importance for our analysis we run individual time series in order to be quite sure we do not have a confounded effect. Though the time series, as we would expect, do not always pick up a conflict effect, they do so on a sufficient number of occasions to convince us that the initiation and termination of interstate conflict do indeed drive military expenditure both up and down.[27]

The fourth and final part of our analysis of interstate conflict concerns its relationship to domestic conflict insofar as that bears on military expenditure.[28] Our main preoccupation is to return to an issue raised in the previous chapter, where we observed that one factor that could account for the relatively weak impact of domestic conflict on military expenditure was what we termed a 'crowding-out' effect of interstate on domestic conflict. To check this very distinct possibility we need quite simply to regress relative military expenditure on the dummies profiling both domestic and interstate conflict. If there is a 'crowding-out' effect then domestic conflict would appear as a more powerful predictor in the multiple rather than the simple equations. This does not happen, leading us to conclude that our previous findings for domestic conflict stand and are not artificially, as it were, weakened due to a 'crowding-out' effect from interstate conflict.[29]

As a corollory we look for an interaction effect between domestic and interstate conflict. Clearly, as far as military expenditure is concerned, domestic conflict is massively less important than interstate conflict. It is conceivable, however, that domestic conflict may be of some greater importance for those countries simultaneously confronting both domestic and interstate conflict. Tests incorporating an interaction effect yield, however, no significant results.[30]

Summary

The principle objective of this chapter has been to explore the relationship between interstate conflict and military expenditure, in which context our general hypothesis has predicted a positive relationship from the former to the latter. More specifically, and primarily to convince ourselves that we are testing for a real relation, we have hypothesized that military expenditure will rise and fall around interstate conflict and will rise differentially in response to the intensity of conflict.

The relationship we have tried to model between conflict and military expenditure is in our view, its rather simple format notwithstanding, really rather complicated. Though some will doubtlessly maintain that our results are patently obvious, these results strike us as not only not obvious but also for both technical and non-technical reasons far from straightforward.

Though we are far from convinced that we have watertight findings, we are, nonetheless, reasonably confident that our general working hypothesis is relatively strongly and pleasingly corroborated. The most general finding is that interstate conflict does indeed stimulate military expenditure and that it does so in a rather dramatic manner. More specifically, while military expenditure rises substantially in response to conflict, it also declines again, assuming the non-recurrence of conflict, in what we have termed the decay effect. This decay only becomes apparent, however, some time after the cesation of the conflict, which gives rise to what we have called the continuation effect. Furthermore, military expenditure appears to be sensitive to the intensity of conflict, as profiled both in duration and level. From those core results we draw the following inferences or implications.

First, interstate conflict appears to influence military expenditure in a rather standardized manner, in that the influence seems to be relatively uniform across different countries. Thus, irrespective of variations in political or economic or social orientation across states, involvement in war appears to elicit a highly homogeneous response as far as military expenditure is concerned. War, in this respect, seems to be a great equalizer.

Second, the impact of interstate conflict on military expenditure seems to be rather dramatic in inducing a quantum increase, which in turn indicates a form of dual modality in the behaviour of military expenditure. Emphasizing that we are dealing explicitly with a partial and not a univariate explanation, we do see military expenditure generally speaking following two quite different modes. The non-conflict and interstate conflict modes are separated by some considerable distance as far as levels of military expenditure are concerned. Though non-conflict states do not of course maintain identical levels of military expenditure, they do, other things being equal, move within a relatively narrow band. Involvement in interstate conflict shatters this band pushing military expenditure through a non-conflict ceiling to levels to which it would otherwise never begin to approximate. It is not so much that interstate conflict increases military spending but induces a quantum leap. States choosing to engage in armed conflict appear therefore to be willing to accept a level of commitment to military expenditure that is qualitatively different from the normal or non-conflict mode.

Third, war does not appear to institutionalize higher levels of military expenditure. While there is a continuation effect, compatible with the idea of institutionalization, such an effect is subject, in the not too long term, to a more powerful decay effect. Assuming the conflict does not reoccur, military expenditure appears to fall to the point that it becomes impossible to distinguish post-conflict from non-conflict states. This is a further indication that war, as far as military expenditure behaviour is concerned, is abnormal.

Although interstate conflict is far from being the modal form of behaviour as far as frequency of occurrence is concerned, it is also not truly exceptional. Thus, just over half of our population of Third World states has experienced some form of interstate conflict, and though the frequency is not increasing there is evidence of some increase in the intensity of conflict. Our fourth inference is that this does not fit happily with North–South models.

One common aproach to such a model is to aggregate any of a variety of economic indicators, such as per capita income or per capita energy consumption, across countries of the so-called North and South. Mean values produced from such aggregations seemingly indicate a substantial gap. Further corroboration for such a gap is seen to lie in a variety of political organizations associated with the North and South alike, such as the OECD group or the Non-Aligned Movement. The implication then is that the North and South constitute different political and economic groups, which are distinctive in terms of their separate common interests and identity. Since a substantial gap is seen to separate these two groups, then it is also frequently assumed that the different interests and identity of the North and South alike are at odds. On a number of scores North–South models seem to us to perpetrate an excessive degree of simplification and, consequently and more seriously, misrepresentation, due to over-aggregation. To give but one illustration, were standard deviations consulted as readily as mean values, then recourse may not be made quite so readily to gap positions. The illustration that is, however, most pertinent to our concerns is derived from our descriptive statistics on interstate conflict. Our descriptive findings are sufficient to indicate that many Third World countries maintain relations with one another which are sufficiently hostile to belie rather the notion of common interests and identity on which much North–South thinking is based. In fact, intra Third World conflict would appear to us to be sufficiently extensive that rather than constituting a diversion from Third World identity it actually constitutes a factor that contributes to an explanation for the absence of such an identity.

A fifth conclusion concerns our view that military expenditure is a response to interstate conflict and as such a means of pursuing war rather than a cause of war. The issue of the appropriate directionality between war and military expenditure is, in our opinion, extremely troublesome. Nonetheless, on three sets of reasons, we have some confidence in inferring military expenditure as a response.

In the first instance, though we would not deny that there are links from the military to war, we generally regard these links as indirect. Thus, for example, it is impossible to conduct an interstate war without a military, but in this context we see the military as a necessary precondition rather than a causal factor. Or again, it is possible to see the military as a factor than can institutionalize tensions between states. Thus, even if military forces are deployed defensively, following some form of deterrence logic, any such defensive positioning still depends ultimately on the maintenance of means of aggression. In this respect, even the most passive deployment of the military can be seen as constituting a threat or tension. Nonetheless, we tend to see the military as something which reinforces rather than originates important tensions and conflicts of interest. Or again, it would be surprising if some calculation on military expenditure did not influence decisions to engage in war. However, we suspect that such calculations would not only be conducted across two or more states (i.e. it would not be any one state's level of military expenditure that was critical but its level relative to other states) but also such calculations would more likely influence the timing rather than the occurrence of war.

While the connections from military expenditure to war seem to us rather indirect, our second grounds for inferring military expenditure as a response are that there seem to be more persuasive arguments positing directionality from war to military expenditure. These derive essentially from a conceptualization of war. Thus, we take war to be first and foremost a subset of conflict, which differs from other subsets principally in terms of variables, such as the means by which or the environment in which conflict is pursued. Not all conflicts of course result in the use of force. Consequently, though the ultimate explanation of war must derive from an explanation of conflict, any satisfactory theory of war must also be able to explain why force is employed as the means of attempted conflict resolution. This in turn entails an identification of those factors that lead two or more parties to conclude, against a given conflict of interests, that greater net gains or lower net losses can be achieved by mutual agreement to use force rather than any other means of conflict resolution. Though we have most assuredly not produced a theory of war, which would we admit be a prerequisite for a firm adherence to our response conclusion, it does seem to us that war is more profitably and fruitfully conceptualized as a function of the conjunction of conflicts of interest and of the mutual perception of the greater gains or lower losses of conflict resolution through force than as a function of a substantially more superficial variable such as military expenditure.

Our third set of reasons derives from our results. Though emphasizing again that we are not without reservations, our findings do seem to us to corroborate a military expenditure as response conclusion. As we have argued in more detail above, levels of military expenditure seem to vary systematically with intensity of conflict, defined either in terms of duration or form. Or again, our findings on continuation and decay effects seem to be more comprehensible when military expenditure is interpreted as a response.

Our sixth conclusion pertains to the qualitative change in levels of militay expenditure induced, other things being equal, by interstate conflict. The war-induced quantum leap, as Cobden noted over a hundred years ago, is in one respect quite bizarre or irrational. If two parties have agreed to engage in a violent resolution of a conflict, they may achieve, other things being equal, exactly the same outcome without both undertaking a quantum increase in military expenditure and experiencing thereby the massive additional opportunity costs. That Cobdenite rationality is not pursued tells us something rather important about the nature of interstate conflict.

Cobdenite rationality may be defeated by any or all of the following factors. The conflicting parties may engage in misperception or miscalculation. Thus, any one party may perceive it could achieve a substantial advantage by increasing its capabilities relative to the other side while failing to appreciate that the other side may make exactly the same calculation. Or again, the Cobdenite prescription presupposes a degree of co-operation that is unlikely to be present in the kind of circumstance where agreement, again ironically a form of co-operation, has been made to engage in mutual violence. Violence, in other words, would seem to preclude otherwise rational forms of conduct. Or again, Cobden may be confounded because of a widespread perception that violent conflict is qualitatively different from other forms of conflict. Parties engaging in violent conflict may well perceive such conflict, precisely because of its forceful nature, to be of a zero-sum character. While actual outcomes may well not prove to be zero-sum, this may not be the dominant perception at the initiation of the conflict simply because the outcome could be zero-sum. Furthermore, the actual process of the conflict itself can entail a zero-sum form of destruction. On these grounds, then, it would be quite rational for each party to commit the maximum possible level of resources to avoid being on the zero end, as it were, of the conflict.

Though we have generally argued, albeit noting some indirect effects, that military expenditure is a response to interstate conflict, we would also argue that war, or more accurately the possibility of war, and a commitment to the military, as opposed to specific levels of military expenditure, are reciprocally related. From this reciprocity we draw our final inference or implication that a commitment to the military perpetrates a self-fulfilling prophecy.

While seeing levels of military expenditure as a response to war, war can only be pursued through the opposition of military forces, in which respect the military, quite tautologically, is a prerequisite of war. As long as states maintain military forces, one of whose principal utilities is to respond to armed conflict, then states are likely to entertain the possibility of conflict resolution through these forces. As long as this possibility exists, then states are likely to infer that they in turn need to retain a military. We appear, therefore, to be in a vicious circle, in which the existence of the military permits a particular form of conflict resolution, namely war, which in turn justifies or demands the continued existence and maintenance of military forces. Thus, while in one respect the military constitutes simply the means of conflict, rather than an immediate explanation of conflict, the very nature of the means does in fact explain the possibility of or potential for war. Since a very obvious response to this possibility, though certainly not the only one, is in fact to continue to maintain a military, then the military has in effect written out its own self-fulfilling justification.

Notes

1. For a selection of analyses reflecting the extremely varied approaches to the topic, see: N. Alcock, *The War Disease* (Ontario: Canadian Peace Research Institute, 1971); G. Blainey, *The Causes of War* (London: Macmillan, 1973); A. Buchan, *War in Modern Society* (London: Collins, 1968); R. Gilpin, *War and Change in World Politics* (Cambridge: Cambridge University Press, 1981); B.B. de Mesquita, *The War Trap* (New Haven: Yale University Press, 1981); M. Midlarsky, *On War* (New York: Free Press, 1975); J.D. Singer and M. Small, *The Wages of War* (New York: Wiley, 1972); Q. Wright, *A Study of War* (Chicago: Chicago University Press, 1965).
2. See for convenient and clear reviews: D.A. Zinnes, 'Why War? Evidence on the Outbreak of International Conflict', in T.R. Gurr (ed.), *Handbook of Political Conflict* (New York: Free Press, 1980); and B.B. de Mesquita, 'Theories of International Conflict' in ibid.
3. We would not of course need to be reminded that our measurement of interstate conflict is relatively crude. That it is so would not perturb us if it is the case that the measurement is both valid and reliable. For our purposes we do not think there is a serious validity problem principally because we are dealing with a rather direct measure. It is true that other things being equal we would prefer an interval measure but such a measure does not exist. Furthermore we consider for the type of effect, for which we wish to test, that an ordinal measure is quite adequate. This measure does at least provide us with an admittedly rather rudimentary measure of intensity but we suspect that we are dealing with a rather rudimentary phenomenon. On the reliability front we suspect that there are no serious problems. Interstate conflict is a readily

recognizable phenomenon and as such widely reported. Furthermore our relatively unelaborate classification reduces classification problems. The sources, from which we have produced the classification, are *Keesings Contemporary Archives* and *Europa Yearbooks*.

4. Table 7.1 is based on aggregated five-year files. In other words countries would be classified as having experienced interstate conflict if they have experienced conflict in any of the designated five years. Some countries may have experienced several different levels of conflict over the designated period. To prevent double-counting, countries that have experienced conflict are classified by their highest level. Levels 1–4 refer to the definitions provided in the Introduction to this chapter.

5. The complications with small numbers of cases in some early years is so extreme that several categories have no cases at all. Since we use more variables in modelling level of interstate conflict, we need to note the adjusted R^2 values. These are respectively for the simple and multiple dummy regressions: 0.28 and 0.26 (1954), 0.17 and 0.17 (1958), 0.28 and 0.26 (1966), 0.17 and 0.19 (1970), 0.39 and 0.49 (1974). 0.08 and 0.13 (1978), 0.09 and 0.11 (1982).

6. The selection of five years is admittedly rather arbitrary on our part. We need a period of time sufficiently long for a contribution effect to manifest itself but not so long that it would have decayed. While the selection of five years is rather arbitrary, we do work below with other selections. The decision to measure the independent variable over five years changes the size of the population slightly as we now exclude those countries that have not been independent over the whole five-year period. We have checked to ensure that this does not disturb our analysis. In addition to a continuation effect, there could also be a build-up effect, which would have much the same consequences, i.e. countries having higher levels of expenditure but not actually engaged as yet in conflict. We could model this by including a variable which measures whether a conflict takes place after the year in which military expenditure is measured. We do not do this partly because we are reticent about modelling future events and partly because we begin to acquire too many independent variables. If there were to be a build-up effect, however, it would not only be consistent with our overall reasoning but would also strengthen our results.

7. The first three equations are clearly troublesome, though troublesome in a coherent manner. Part of the problem unquestionably pertains to the small number of cases experiencing conflict, which for some categories is in fact zero. The absences of significant equations for the simple dummy regressions in 1954 and 1958 are explained by the lower military expenditure values of conflict levels beyond that of border skirmishes. 1962 is dominated by conflicts of the border skirmish variety. Had these sorts of results endured we would have been in difficulty. However, from the period 1962–66 as both the number of cases increases and the distribution over levels of conflict improves, then results move into line with our expectations. The adjusted R^2 values for the simple and multiple dummy equations are: 0.33 and 0.30 (1966), 0.25 and 0.26 (1970), 0.35 and 0.49 (1974), 0.21 and 0.31 (1978), 0.11 and 0.14 (1982).

8. In a number of years analyses of residuals show outlier problems. We have therefore excluded the following in the following years: S. Vietnam (1962); Burma, Saudi Arabia and Iraq (1966); Iraq and Oman (1970); Mauritania and Saudi Arabia (1978); Saudi Arabia (1982).

9. For example, if we run a simple Kendal's tau test for zero conflict category against time we find a positive correlations of 0.76, i.e. the zero category does increase its level

of relative military expenditure over time. A similar correlation for the lower conflict category yields a correlation of −0.05, i.e. there is no propensity for this category to increase its level of military spending over time.

10. The interval variable has the advantage over the set of dummies of increasing our degrees of freedom. It has two disadvantages. First, the set of dummies enables us to model better the break, which is not continuous, between some and no conflict. Second, the set of dummies enables us to examine whether we get any marked, i.e. not continuous changes, as we go from any number of years to another.

11. We are more or less bound to find a significant relationship of some kind between military expenditure and years of conflict precisely because there is a relationship of military expenditure to conflict. Thus, even if military expenditure were invariant across years, there would still be a positive relationship, though a much weaker one than that of military expenditure to conflict. In order to claim that there is a real year effect we need first to check that the level of explained variation does not drop substantially and that values of military expenditure increase across years. Since both these conditions hold we conclude there is a real duration effect.

12. The constants vary across the two sets of equations in Table 7.5 because when military expenditure is regressed on duration as a continuous variable the constant is not the true mean value of the non-conflict category which is the case for the dummy regressions. In this respect the dummy regressions are the more desirable, though they do incur the difficulty of using more degrees of freedom. Comparisons of adjusted R^2 values indicates that both sets of results are very similar. The adjusted values for the continuous and dummy forms are: 0.48 and 0.48 (1966), 0.43 and 0.42 (1970), 0.36 and 0.36 (1974), 0.28 and 0.30 (1978), 0.22 and 0.22 (1982). The dummy results do show up some weaknesses though they generally indicate strong linearity. Finally, we may note that the dummy regressions illustrate well the kind of discontinuity created by conflict in that the coefficient for the first dummy is always higher than the coefficient for the continuous measure.

13. The lack of independence, meaning that if a country has experienced conflict then duration must be of one year or more, has been discussed in a footnote above. Including both duration and level into a regression equation does therefore create collinearity problems, which is unfortunate as regressing military expenditure on both of these variables is much the easiest way to assess the relative importance of either. This difficulty can however be overcome by combining the variables. Thus, four dummy or categoric variables are constructed in terms of: (a) presence of low-level conflict of 2 years' duration or less, (b) presence of low-level conflict of 3–5 years' duration, (c) presence of high-level conflict of 2 years' duration or less, (d) presence of high-level conflict of 3–5 years. The acronyms for each of these variables are respectively: 12−, 13+, 22−, 23+. A regression of relative military expenditure on each of these variables is in effect a regression on the mean level of each category in which the constant term is the mean for the non-conflict.

14. The acronyms for Table 7.6 are explained in the previous note. The initial absence of significant equations does not disturb us as there is a shortage of cases. There are, however, some undesired results in that b coefficients do not always conform to a consistent pattern.

15. For the years for which we have significant equations, the movement from shorter to longer duration in the low conflict category increases military expenditure on average by 1.4 times. the analagous movement in the high-conflict category increases expenditure by 2.4 times.

16. Other things being equal, we might expect the impact of a conflict to be greater at time t rather than t minus say five years. We have not as yet controlled for this problem. Thus we are modelling a time effect on the basis that the impact at t minus five would be the same as at t. If this is indeed not the case, then the impact of duration would be less than it should be. We have furthermore something of a confounded effect in that duration does to some extent measure timing of the conflict. Thus if we have a duration score of five years, then conflict must of necessity be taking place in the year of measurement of military expenditure, whereas if duration is one year then the conflict may happen in the year of measurement of military expenditure or in any of the preceding five years.

17. As in the case of duration there will almost inevitably be some relationship of military expenditure to decay simply because the two variables are not independent. Again, however, the strength and direction of the relationship is not predetermined. Decay as a continuous variable is measured such that zero equals no conflict, one equals conflict ceased five years ago, to five which equals conflict is continuing. In other words, a positive relationship of military expenditure to decay indicates a decay effect. It may seem odd to score decay such that a decay effect yields a positive rather than a negative sign. We do this principally because we wish to preserve zero for the no-conflict category. When decay is measured as a set of dummies, each dummy represents a measure of the last year of conflict. As above for duration, five dummies model six categories with the no-conflict category being represented by the constant.

18. When relative military expenditure is regressed on decay as a continuous variable we achieve significant equations in all test years from 1958–62 to 1978–82. The coefficients and R^2 values are respectively: 0.06 and 0.12 (1962); 0.11 and 0.41 (1966); 0.12 and 0.29 (1970); 0.12 and 0.38 (1974); 0.08 and 0.20 (1978); 0.07 and 0.14 (1982). Antilogging any coefficient multiplied by the number of years would provide a significant estimate of the magnitude of decay. Thus, for example, for the 1958–62 test period a continuing conflict would significantly predict to a level of expenditure double that of no-conflict category whereas a conflict that terminated five years earlier would predict to a level 1.15 times the no-conflict category. The dummy regressions produce only marginally better R^2 values once we adjust for degrees of freedom. Generally speaking, there is the same continuity in increases in values of the coefficients as the hostility becomes more contemporaneous. As we would expect given earlier results, the dummy variables model slightly better the discontinuity between no and some conflict.

19. Over the five-year analysis we construct four dummy variables defined in terms of low and high conflict (indicated 1 and 2) and termination set at more than three years and less than three years prior to the measurement of military expenditure (indicated 2– and 3+). This gives acronyms of: 12–, 13+, 22–, and 23+. For the nine-year analysis, low and high conflict are similarly organized across three-year spans where 1–3, 4–6, 7–9 years are indicated D1, D2, D3. This gives six dummy variables, where for example 1D1 means presence of low-level conflict that terminated in the first three years of the nine year period.

20. For example, focusing on the nine-year results we may consider the equations for the five test years for which we have significant results. If we now take initially the low-conflict categories and aggregate the number of significant and insignificant coefficients across the 1–3, 4–6, 7–9 year bands, then we find ratios of: 0 to 5 (1–3), 2 to 3 (4–6), 3 to 2 (7–9). The matching ratios for the high conflict category are: 0 to 3 (1–3), 3 to 1 (4–6), and 5 to 0 (7–9).

21. We check this by running individual time series for all countries where military expenditure is regressed on time and conflict. If conflict always increased expenditure abruptly and then equally abruptly on termination reduced expenditure, then dummy measures of conflict would always produce significant estimators. This does admittedly happen but more often than not a dummy measure does not prove significant.

22. It might also be argued that the decay effect we see is not due, as we argue, to any decline in expenditure after conflict has terminated but in fact to what we might call a 'leapfrog' effect. By this we mean countries committing themselves to war might progressively over time move up the level of military expenditure at which they engage in war. This 'leapfrog' interpretation would in fact fit with the type of progressive results we get in any one test year. However, if the 'leapfrog' interpretation were correct, then it would have to continue across test years, which it very explicitly does not. Countries engaging in interstate conflict are unequivocally not moving up over time the level of military expenditure at which they engage in interstate conflict.

23. While there may well be a military build-up prior to war, which admittedly may do nothing to reduce tensions, we would not equate any such build-up with the causes of the war.

24. For instance it seems to us decidedly more likely that border skirmishes develop due to such factors as competing territorial claims rather than two states arriving at particular levels of military expenditure. We can envisage that border skirmishes can develop into more major conflicts. However, again we would see this as a result of competing parties being inadvertently unable to contain the conflict or deliberately escalating it rather than simply being unable, as it were, to turn off any rise in military expenditure.

25. If high levels of military expenditure did sensitize states to a more ready use of conflict, then the decay in expenditure after conflict could only be explained by a substantial change in behaviour on the part of such states. War would have a truly profound influence on state behaviour in that it would desensitize aggressive behaviour. This would mean for those states for which conflict reappears that they would go through substantial shifts in learning, unlearning, relearning etc.

26. Two examples of immediate relevance to us may be noted. First, cross-sectional analysis could obscure a conflict effect if it were the case that only smaller expenditure countries engaged in conflict and did not raise their expenditure to levels higher than the highest spenders. Though this is possible, it would be an unusual situation. Furthermore, our results are sufficiently powerful that we can hardly be said to have obscured results. This in effect happens, we would argue, because conflict raises expenditure to such high levels that it goes beyond the limits of 'normal' expenditure. Second, it is possible even though we may document decay that military expenditure may be high prior to the conflict for a reason other than the conflict itself. Though this seems unlikely to us on any consistent basis, a solution in part is to run individual time series.

27. Individual time series, where relative military expenditure is regressed on time and dummies for conflict, indicate that conflict is a significant estimator in a large number of cases. This could only happen if conflict both increased and, on cessation, decreased levels of expenditure. It does not happen in all cases in which respect we should emphasize that time series can obscure effects also. Thus, time series results could be undermined by build-up or continuation effects; time series have more limited degrees of freedom; variations in expenditure during a conflict could

weaken dummy measures; variation in time series is often less than in cross-sectional analysis; or time series particularly if conflict moved expenditure up to roughly similar levels across all cases would pick up an effect more readily in smaller than larger military spenders. The combination of the cross-sectional and time series results are sufficient, however, to lead us to be quite confident in asserting that we do have our hypothesized causal rise and fall in expenditure around conflict.

28. Although our main concern is purely with the relationship of domestic to interstate conflict as this influence estimates of military expenditure, we may note a small detour on the immediate relationship of domestic to interstate conflict. The subject of the so-called nexus of interstate and domestic conflict has attracted substantial attention and substantial variation in results. Generally, domestic conflict is taken to predict to interstate conflict on either of two grounds. Either the occurrence of domestic conflict leads a neighbour to initiate an interstate conflict on the grounds that the state experiencing domestic conflict would be vulnerable. Or the state experiencing domestic would itself initiate interstate conflict on account of some scapegoat reasoning (such as to detract attention from domestic problems or stimulate domestic solidarity). These two explanations both predict from domestic to interstate conflict but differ only in who initiates the conflict. In other words we can test for the validity of each by examining whether a relationship holds from domestic to interstate conflict. If such a test were positive, we would then decide between the two explanations in terms of who was responsible for initiating the conflict. Commonly this association is tested through correlation analysis or some variant thereof such as factor analysis. This seems to us entirely inappropriate as whichever explanation we pursued would contain a large number of cases which experienced interstate but not domestic conflict. In fact if all wars were simply dyadic then half the cases of interstate conflict would not experience domestic conflict. The more appropriate relationship is not a simple correlation between domestic and interstate conflict but between the conditional probabilities of non-occurrence and occurrence of interstate conflict given domestic conflict. More precisely we would expect the probability of no interstate conflict given domestic conflict to approximate to zero and the conditional probability of interstate given domestic conflict to approximate to one. This is unequivocally not the case. Domestic conflict is overwhelmingly more likely to result in no interstate conflict. That there is some overlap between domestic and interstate conflict cannot be taken to corroborate even a partial relationship since unless we posited an inverse as opposed to an independent relationship between domestic and interstate conflict we would expect there to be some overlap. For a good and thorough survey of this literature, see: M. Stohl, 'The Nexus of Civil and International Conflict', in T.R. Gurr (ed.), *Handbook of Political Conflict*, op.cit.

29. In only one test year (1970) does domestic conflict become significant, controlling for interstate conflict, on an occasion where without the control it was insignificant. We repeat the procedure on a more elaborate scale using the five-year files, where we incorporate a range of domestic conflict variables (number of years of domestic conflict, number of years of sustained domestic conflict, number of years of organized conflict) and a range of interstate variables (presence of low or high conflict, number of years of conflict). Again, we can find no evidence of any 'crowding-out' effect.

30. We obtain an interaction term using a dummy coded one for cases experiencing both domestic and interstate conflict. Relative military expenditure is now regressed on domestic conflict, interstate conflict and domestic plus interstate conflict. The first two variables could indicate an additive effect but only the last could tell us if there is

an interactive effect. A comparison of the three variable interactive equations against the two variable additive equations across all test years shows that the interactive term is never significant. In fact the R^2 values never change by more than a point or two, while the technically more correct focus on adjusted R^2 values of course shows a small reduction. The inclusion of an interactive term in more elaborate equations for the five-year files again shows no significant interactive results.

8 Military Expenditure and National Security

Introduction

While maintaining from the last chapter an interstate focus, we turn our attention now from direct conflict to what we might call a conflict-related area. More specifically this conflict related area is defined by the problematique of national security, which we take in turn to hinge in important part on the so-called security dilemma. Before outlining our general working hypothesis, which seeks to connect security calculations to military expenditure, we outline the set of assumptions, which constitutes our rationale, through several stages.

The first stage pertains to a conceptualization of security, which we take, quite conventionally, to be a variable phenomenon, meaning it can exist to greater or lesser degrees, defined in terms of the relative absence of threats.[1] Insecurity, which means quite simply low-level security, we take to be a function on the one hand of the perception of a threat, in turn a function of the damage or harm that can be inflicted on what are taken to be vital interests, and on the other hand of the perceived ability to respond to the threat. Holding constant capacity to respond, insecurity will increase as threat perception increases; equally, holding constant threat perception, insecurity will increase as capacity to respond reduces. Thus, any actor will enjoy a high level of security if it has a highly developed capacity to promote and protect what it takes to be its vital interests in the environment in which it finds itself.

Insecurity can take a variety of different substantive forms, corresponding to the substantive form of vital interests being threatened. Furthermore, insecurity can be manifested across a range of different levels from individuals upwards. Our preoccupation is primarily with military security at the state level, though many of the points we now make are readily translatable to other levels and other substantive areas.[2]

The second stage confronts the issue of how military capabilities impinge on each of the twin factors, threat to interests and response to threat, whose interplay defines levels of security. The connections in each case, we suggest, are both strong and direct.

The connection to threat derives from the association of capabilities to power. Capabilities strongly influence power relations both indirectly by virtue of setting parametres within which interactions take place or directly by being employed in a coercive capacity. Though military capabilities are certainly not the sole source of power, they unquestionably constitute an impressive threat on a variety of different scores. The basis of military power is force, which is impressive as a threat both in the immediacy and extensiveness of the damage it can inflict on vital interests. Moreover, national militaries represent extremely visible and large constellations of force. Furthermore, national militaries are deployed in an area in which force is held by many observers to be the ultimate arbiter of conflicts and interests. Other things being equal, any one state may eminently reasonably look to the military capabilities of other states and interpret these as very real potential threats.[3]

Any one state is not of course paralysed or powerless in such a situation and has the option of making a response. This response of course is in turn its option of developing its military capabilities. Other things being equal, then, holding constant threat any state can increase its security by expanding its military capabilities.

Thus military capabilities are both the source of and response to threat. It is the reciprocal relationship between these two factors that constitutes the so-called security dilemma. Any state can readily increase its military security but only, other things being equal, at the expense of reducing the security of others.[4]

Summarizing the main assumptions thus far, we would posit that military capabilities constitute both a source of and means of reducing insecurity. Since the capabilities of any one state have little meaning or relevance except in comparison to those of other states, then military security must be comparative or relative. We assume, therefore, that states engage in security calculations, by which we mean states juxtapose their capabilities against those of other states in their environment.

The third and final stage of our rationale draws on some empirical results from Chapter 3. If, as we assume, states make security calculations in response to their military environment, two questions raise themselves: how is this environment defined and to what in the military environment is a response being made.

Reiterating, though recasting slightly, some of the results of Chapter 3 have already examined one possible environment, which we may term global, and two possible responses, which we may term relative and absolute. The analysis of Chapter 3 is global in the sense that it focuses on all Third World countries. In principle at least this seems a realistic assumption to the extent that states are aware of an international hierarchy and are concerned to maintain their position in that hierarchy. By an absolute response we mean that states take cognisance of the gross or absolute capabilities of other states. This seems eminently plausible on what we might term 'battlefield' grounds. By this we mean that, other things being equal, the outcomes of battles, i.e. actual displays of force, would be strongly predicted by the ratio of the absolute capabilities of the conflicting states. By a relative response we mean that states take cognisance not of the gross but relative military capabilities of other states. Though this would be irrational from a 'battlefield' perspective, states may adopt this response because they attach significance to the military burden or military commitment of other states. In effect then the military burden or commitment would become a measure of aggressive or threatening intent.

The results from Chapter 3 provide no empirical corroboration for a global response of either absolute or relative form.[5] This could indicate that our whole line of reasoning on comparative security calculations is invalid. A less damning criticism, however, would be that the reasoning is valid but that we selected the wrong level of environment. The ensuing analysis consequently shifts the environment from a global to a neighbourhood level.[6] In principal, at least, this seems to us a plausible change in that while Third World states may be well aware of a global hierarchy, they may be substantially more preoccupied with their immediate neighbours for the simple reason that they are as yet unable to threaten or be threatened by states outside their neighbourhood. The dubious privilege of being able to threaten or be threatened outside a neighbourhood is something which, as yet, is peculiar to a small number of high-income countries – Brazil and India as yet do not have the means to become enemies.

We are finally in a position to stipulate our general working hypothesis, which is that the level of any one state's military expenditure is a function, other things being equal, of its response through a military security calculation to the security threat, operationalized by levels of military expenditure, posed by the states constituting its neighbourhood environment. More specifically we test two hypotheses differentiated in terms of whether the response or accommodation is directed at absolute or relative levels of expenditure in the neighbourhood environment.

Findings

The first variant of our general working hypothesis focuses on an absolute accommodation where we reason that any one state in setting its level of military expenditure is influenced by the gross or absolute expenditures of its neighbours. Such a security calculation would then be based on what we term a 'battlefield' reasoning. Generally speaking variation in size across countries is sufficiently great that we would argue that it is unrealistic for a test of this hypothesis to expect that all countries in a neighbourhood would develop their military capabilities to exactly the same absolute levels. We would however expect that there should be clear movement in this direction. Consequently, we hypothesize that, in any neighbourhood, states would adjust their absolute expenditures through a process of mutual compensation so as to achieve some degree of equalization. Restating this in a form more amenable to testing, we would expect smaller states in any neighbour to commit proportionately more of their GDP to the military. This it should be noted would not of necessity produce absolute parity in any neighbourhood, which we taken to be an unrealistic and unreasonable test, but it would indicate movement towards equalization, which we would require for minimum corroboration.

To test this hypothesis we take each individual neighbourhood and rank states in that neighbourhood by GDP and by relative military expenditure levels. If our hypothesis is to be corroborated, then we would expect to find negative correlations between these ranks. In other words we would be finding that smaller countries committed more of their GDP to the military than larger countries and consequently though absolute levels in the neighbourhood would not of necessity be of parity they would be moving in that direction.

Using Kendall's tau, a non-parametic test in our view ideally suited to our purposes, we initially sum for tau across all neighbourhoods. Table 8.1 presents these results for the 1978 test year.[7] These results provide absolutely no corroboration for our hypothesis.[8]

Table 8.1: Details of Kendall's tau for correlation between ranked GDP and relative military expenditure by neighbourhood size, 1978

Tau details	Neighbourhood size							
	2	3	4	5	6	7	8	9
N	8	22	17	11	11	5	2	3
Sigma S	0	−13	0	6	−3	−1	26	4
Sigma Tau N	8	66	102	110	165	105	56	108
Sigma Tau	0.00	−0.20	0.00	0.05	−0.02	0.00	0.46	0.03

Though Table 8.1 is a legitimate, though perhaps slightly unusual, application of tau, it does potentially contain a major blunder. There is, it seems to us, a plausible alternative to our hypothesis which would postulate mutual divergence rather than mutual compensation. This alternative would predict a positive relationship between the rankings of GDP and relative military expenditure, indicating that larger states proportionately committed more to the military, thereby enhancing the gap in absolute capabilities. The results in Table 8.1 unequivocally demonstrate that there is no corroboration either for this alternative hypothesis. The potential blunder is that we could get the results of Table 8.1 if each relationship held across an approximately equal number of countries. In other words we would be wrong to conclude that absolute accommodation did not take place. Rather we should conclude that such accommodation does take place, albeit in two diametrically opposed forms in two different categories of neighbourhoods. It would then be contingent on us to identify what differentiated these two categories of neighbourhoods.

In order to check this problem we need to deal with scores across individual neighbourhoods rather than the population of aggregated neighbourhoods. This raises a number of difficulties, which we discuss in footnotes.[9] However, the results from Tables 8.2 and 8.3 indicate that we are not confounding significant positive and negative findings.

We are confident in concluding therefore that states do not adjust their levels of military expenditure to accommodate to the absolute levels of expenditure of their neighbours.

The second variant of our general working hypothesis focuses again on the idea of an accommodative response built on neighbourhood security calculations

Table 8.2: Frequency of tau values for neighbourhoods of two and three members, 1978

Tau value	frequency	
	Two members	Three members
−1.00	4	5
−0.33	—	10
0.33	—	4
1.00	4	3

Table 8.3: Frequency of tau values for neighbourhoods with membership greater than three, 1978

	Tau values										
	0.00	0.01–0.10	0.11–0.20	0.21–0.30	0.31–0.40	0.41–0.50	0.51–0.60	0.61–0.70	0.71–0.80	0.81–0.90	0.91–1.00
Positive	7	3	3	1	10	3	0	2	0	0	1
Negative	—	4	3	0	7	0	1	2	0	0	3

but anticipates that the response is made in relative rather than absolute terms. We hypothesize, therefore, that states in any neighbourhood will develop their military capabilities such that their levels of relative military expenditure approximate to parity. Again we would hold that to require perfect parity would be unrealistic; we would demand that movement towards parity would be required for minimum corroboration.

We elaborate our test results through four stages. The first of these considers all possible dyads, where a dyad is any two neighbouring countries. Each state is categorized in terms of an above or below status, where these two status levels are defined in terms of whether a state has a positive or negative residual from an overall regression of military expenditure on GDP.[10] In other words, above and below states are respectively spending more or less on their military than we would expect on the basis of their GDP. Any dyad can take any one of three possible combinations: both states above, both below, one above and one below. If military expenditure levels were unrelated, then we would expect combinations of above and below status to be randomly distributed.[11] This expected distribution can be juxtaposed against the actual one. If there is a neighbourhood effect one would expect a mismatch between the expected and actual distributions, indicating a greater propensity for above or below states to cluster. As we see from Table 8.4, we do indeed find a mismatch.[12]

Table 8.4: Frequency of actual and expected dyads by above–above, above–below, below–below status, selected years, 1958–82

Years	Above and below status						N dyads
	Above–above		Above–below		Below–below		
	Actual	Expected	Actual	Expected	Actual	Expected	
1958	10	6	18	21	18	19	46
1962	26	21	32	42	28	22	86
1966	35	26	57	62	33	38	125
1970	37	20	46	63	49	49	132
1974	41	27	52	67	43	42	136
1978	36	27	50	67	50	42	136
1982	42	35	46	60	33	26	121

The second stage turns to neighbourhoods where we calculate the percentage of states in each neighbourhood that are above. Our hypothesis would predict that neighbourhoods would show a marked propensity to symmetry, i.e. neighbours would tend to cluster as symmetrically above or below as opposed to mixed. As we see from Table 8.5 there is indeed a propensity to symmetry. Averaging over all test years, some 60 per cent of all neighbours are symmetrical in the sense of having two-thirds or more of their members as under- or overspenders.

Table 8.5: Percentage of neighbours classified by percentage above in neighbourhood, selected years 1958–82

Years	% Above in neighbourhood					N
	0	1–32	33–67	68–69	100	
1958	24	15	47	6	9	34
1962	15	15	39	13	19	54
1966	18	8	52	11	10	71
1970	28	14	36	7	16	76
1974	23	13	39	10	15	79
1978	22	18	35	6	19	79
1982	13	9	46	11	21	76

The third stage examines the conditional probability that a state will be an overspender given the percentage of its neighbours which are overspenders. Our hypothesis would predict that there should be a tendency for the probability that a state overspends to increase as the percentge of its neighbours that overspends increases. As Table 8.6 documents, this hypothesized tendency is extremely marked. At the extremes, if a state finds itself in a neighbourhood where all its

Table 8.6: Conditional probability of overspending by states given selected sets of percentage of neighbours (PN) that overspend, selected years 1958–82

Percentage of neighbours that overspend	Conditional probability that state overspends						
	1958	1962	1966	1970	1974	1978	1982
PN = 0	0.11	0.11	0.07	0.17	0.18	0.15	0.29
0 > PN < 50	0.33	0.43	0.54	0.20	0.38	0.38	0.43
50 > PN < 100	0.56	0.50	0.52	0.39	0.57	0.45	0.54
PN = 100	0.43	0.91	0.54	0.86	0.67	0.83	0.80

neighbours underspend, the probability, averaged over all test years, that it will overspend is 0.15; conversely, if a state finds itself in a neighbourhood where all its neighbours overspend, the probability that it too will overspend, averaged over all test years, is 0.72.

Thus far, we have dealt with states or neighbourhoods purely in terms of above and below status. A more stringent test of the second variant of our general working hypothesis, for which we already have some substantial corroboration, focuses on the amount of under- and overspending within neighbourhoods.[13] If we order neighbourhoods in terms of percentage of cases above and calculate the mean balance of under- and overspending, then we would expect the mean balance of overspending and percentage of cases overspending within neighbourhoods to increase together. We focus on the amount of under- and overspending but calculate these amounts separately for below and above countries in each neighbourhood.[14] We hypothesize both that the amount of overspending in overspending countries will increase and that the amount of underspending in underspending countries will reduce as the percentage of above countries within neighbourhoods respectively increases and decreases.[15]

Table 8.7, in our view, contains a set of both interesting and powerful results. We may notice initially that the extent to which states either over- or underspend is, on average, greatest when all other states in the neighbourhood respectively over- or underspend. Furthermore, with just a couple of small exceptions, the amount or degree to which both overspending increases and underspending reduces corresponds neatly with the rise in the percentage of states in a neighbourhood that overspend. There is in other words a scissor type of pattern between the amount of over- and underspending. As the percentage of overspending countries in neighbourhoods reduces, then the amount of overspending by the overspending states will reduce and the extent to which underspending countries underspend will increase. The magnitude of under- and overspending within neighbourhoods is, in other words, systematically related.[16]

Taking these four stages together, we would argue that we have strong corroboration for the second variant of our general working hypothesis, postulating that states react to the levels of relative military expenditure of the other states in their

Table 8.7: Mean number of times that states over- or underspend by over- and underspending groups within neighbourhoods across levels of overspending, selected years 1958–82

Over- and underspending groups by year		Percentage of states within neighbourhood that overspend				
		0	1–33	34–67	68–99	100
1958	Over	—	1.25	1.88	3.82	4.37
	Under	2.62	1.93	1.55	1.57	—
1962	Over	—	1.36	1.59	2.73	2.93
	Under	2.06	1.99	1.75	1.59	—
1966	Over	—	1.37	1.79	2.54	2.99
	Under	2.00	1.72	1.59	1.43	—
1970	Over	—	1.47	1.87	1.88	4.32
	Under	2.06	1.73	1.74	1.31	—
1974	Over	—	1.61	1.96	2.78	4.97
	Under	2.38	2.09	1.43	1.74	—
1978	Over	—	1.66	2.00	2.31	4.14
	Under	2.66	2.07	1.84	1.53	—
1982	Over	—	1.62	1.65	1.91	3.46
	Under	2.66	2.50	2.50	1.91	—

neighbourhood. Not only is it the case that states within neighbourhoods develop a marked degree of symmetry in terms of whether they under- or overspend but also the magnitude of underspending is systematically related by virtue of being a function of the proportion of cases within neighbourhoods that under- or overspend.

Before presenting a summary and evaluation of the implications of our findings, we turn, as in previous chapters, to consider several sets of criticisms that may be levelled against our analysis. One such set would not dispute our findings as such but would question the rationale we have deployed to explain these findings. Rather than invoking the kind of reciprocal military calculation inherent in the security dilemma effect to explain the undisputed harmony in military commitment within neighbourhoods, it could be argued that this harmony is a function of either parallel or contiguous effects. In other words, it would be argued we have the wrong independent variable. Since the cases for what we have termed parallel and contiguous effects, though related, are slightly different, we deal separately with each.

The parallel critique would argue that the similarity in expenditure levels, which we impute to the security dilemma effect, is in fact due to analogous developments taking place simultaneously, or in parallel across neighbouring countries. Such countries may manifest similar expenditure levels not because they are responding to each other but because they are all experiencing, for example, military regimes or domestic conflict or interstate conflict. We have two objections to this position.

First, while there are unquestionably some regional variations, we think it highly unlikely that rather generalized developments, such as military regimes or domestic or interstate conflict, would cluster neatly at different levels of intensity across neighbourhoods to provide the type of results we find. Second, and rather less speculatively, were such variables indeed to cluster by neighbourhood, then they would be collinear with our security dilemmas effect. Though our test results for this problem do not appear until the next chapter, we can report that there is no collinearity. As far as the parallel critique is concerned, we are confident that we do not confound a security dilemma effect with other variables contained in our study, i.e. there is an independent effect. What of course we must concede is that there may well be variables, which we have failed to include in our study, that render our security dilemma effect spurious. Returning, however, to our initial more speculative objection, we think it highly unlikely not that there are additional determinants we have failed to include but that these determinants would cluster in a parallel form.

The contiguous effect would postulate that a development in say one state might raise military expenditure, which in turn would diffuse to neighbouring states. Of the various variables we profile a good candidate for such a type of contiguous demonstration effect would be war. Thus, if two stages engage in war, then it would be possible given the known effect of war on military expenditure, that neighbouring states not engaged in the war itself would increase their levels of military expenditure out of fear they too may be drawn into the conflict.

The reasoning behind a contiguous demonstration effect sounds to us eminently possible, but we take it to be something which is in fact highly compatible with a security dilemma effect. The latter works on the basis that states respond to each other's levels of military expenditure through the harm that can be inflicted on them by the levels of military expenditure of their neighbours. If war raises military expenditure then the security dilemma rationale would in fact predict that it would be entirely rational for adjacent states, not immediately involved in the war, to raise their levels of military expenditure. War in this respect is not something that would render a security dilemma effect spurious but would simply constitute one of the factors that could define the fear or insecurity driving the security dilemma effect. In other words, we would not dispute that war by one state may influence the level of military spending in another state with which it is not in conflict. On the contrary we suggest that if this does indeed happen, it happens precisely through the influence or mediation of a security dilemma effect.

A second set of criticisms would be levelled not at the charge that a security dilemma effect is spurious but that it is an uninteresting tautology. Thus, it might be asserted that to argue that any one state influences the level of military expenditure of its neighbours and vice versa is distinctly uninteresting. Or again, to suggest that some countries spend more relatively than others, because the neighbours of the former spend more than the neighbours of the latter, is tautologous. What is under attack here, then, is not so much the mechanics of our analysis but the logic, interest and importance of the security dilemma reasoning as a whole.

There is undoubtedly an element of circularity in the kind of norm of the level of military expenditure seemingly evolved by contiguous states. This norm is collectively produced by all the states in a neighbourhood and, as such, any one state reciprocally influences and is influenced by the expenditure of its neighbours. This strikes us, however, as an illustration of a reciprocal relationship rather than a tautology.

More importantly, we consider the reasoning behind the security dilemma effect far from being uninteresting to be really quite insightful on the complex nature of security. The essence of the security dilemma argument is that the military represents a double-faced phenomenon. It purportedly both threatens violence to others while offering protection from violence by others. It is the coterminous potential of protection from violence through the organization and mobilization of violence that constitutes the Janus type nature of the military. The catch or, more precisely, the dilemma is that it is impossible while deploying military forces even simply for protective purposes to avoid the possibility of threatening violence.[17] Since violence underpins both the protection and the threat, it is impossible to escape from the security dilemma except by eradicating the source of that dilemma, which in turn would require abolishing the military. The circulatory or double-faced nature of the military, captured wonderfully by the security dilemma, illustrates beautifully yet again the self-fulfilling nature of military systems. We have one of the major explanations for the ubiquity and endurability of military forces, which is something that does not strike us as uninteresting.

A third set of criticisms could be levelled at what we might call the seeming absence of variable predictions from the security dilemma effect. The logic behind the security dilemma reasoning would seem to imply a generalized effect, in the sense that all states would be subjected to a similar pressure, through the maintenance of their military capabilities, of responding to and creating a security threat. However, if states do indeed respond to each other's levels of military expenditure by evolving neighbourhood norms, then why, it may be objected, do we find variability in the level of these norms. More precisely, it could be argued: why do states not evolve a low norm and why do we find some neighbourhoods stacked at much higher levels of military expenditure than others. We would readily concede that the security dilemma phenomenon would be decidedly less interesting if it could not explain in part variability across states.

The first of two responses we have to this line of objection is that too much should not be expected from the security dilemma effect. This effect is most certainly, as we have seen, not the only influence on military expenditure and consequently variation can appear across states due to the differential influence of other determinants. More importantly, however, it is crucial to remember that the security dilemma does not predict a particular level of expenditure for any one state but rather similar levels across that group of states which are responding to each other.

Second, it would seem to us that security dilemma reasoning is amenable to some degree of variability. Implicit in this reasoning is not only competition between states but the possibility for spiral effects through reciprocal competition.[18] In other words, security dilemma reasoning does encompass a dynamic effect and as soon as we have a dynamic effect then we have the possibility of variation. Moving to an empirical level we have profiled the composition of each neighbourhood in terms of the proportions of over- and underspenders at each of our test years and examined the changes over time in these compositions. While we do unquestionably find movement, which we would expect, we also find a strong propensity for movement towards harmony. For example, if one state exists as an underspender in an otherwise overspending neighbourhood it tends to adjust upwards. Or again, the most stable constellations are those neighbourhoods consisting of homogeneously over- and underspending states.[19] It seems to use that the logic of the prisoner dilemma game would explain these dynamics rather well.[20] Thus, one of the inferences we would draw from the co-operation – competition matrix of the prisoner dilemma game is that there is strong pressure for actors to cluster in either the top left or bottom right corners (which in our case would be all under- or all overspenders respectively). Equally, and it may be noted more variably, we might expect mixed neighbourhoods to show lower levels of both over- and underspending than we find in the totally homogeneous neighbourhoods. This, it might be recalled from Table 8.7, is precisely what we do find. In sum, the kind of pressures for movement and indeed even the magnitude of movement that we would expect from prisoner dilemma games seem to fit our results rather well. Incorporating prisoner dilemma logic into the security dilemma appears to us to provide a means for explaining then some degree of variability across neighbourhoods.

A final set of objections, with which we would entirely concur, is that we have employed some assumptions which may be overly simplistic and left some rather obvious and interesting questions unanswered. For instance, we have set neighbourhoods at broadly speaking contiguous states. It is conceivable that neighbourhoods could be larger, or that there might by systematic variation in the appropriate size of neighbourhoods, or more interestingly still that the size of neighbourhood may vary systematically by state (for example, larger sizes may define larger neighbourhoods for themselves than smaller states). Or again, we have assumed that all states in a neighbour are equal. It may well be that some states act as leaders and consequently have a disproportionate influence on any neighbourhood norm. To such criticisms we can only make the rather lame, though nonetheless real, excuse that any project has its limits. We are not worried by such problems as we would see them as essentially refining and strengthening our line of analysis.

Summary

The rationale on which the analysis of this chapter is based stems ultimately from the means of violence inherent in national militaries and more immediately from the double-sided nature of the military as both a source of and response to insecurity. The security dilemma hinges on the contention that the existence of other states' military capabilities constitutes a potential threat to a state, to which it can choose to respond by maintaining or enhancing its own capabilities. This leads to our general working hypothesis that predicts that the level of military expenditure of any state is influenced by the levels of expenditure of those other states that constitute its security environment. More particularly this leads us to expect that states in any security environment will collectively evolve a military expenditure level norm for that environment.

We have tested our general hypothesis by defining an environment in terms of a neighbourhood, and we have looked for responses made in the neighbourhood in terms of both absolute and relative levels of expenditure. Our analysis yields, we would suggest, strong corroboration for the second variant of our general working hypothesis. In other words, states in any neighbourhood do indeed appear to evolve a norm that sets the level of relative military expenditure, or military burden, for that neighbourhood. From this general result we draw the following implications.

The first concerns the implication of states responding to relative rather than absolute levels of expenditure. Both measures of expenditure operationalize something to do with security but they operationalize rather different facets of security. Absolute expenditure, the measure to which a response appears not to be made, operationalizes what we have termed a 'battlefield' capability. Other things being equal, we would take a battlefield capability to be critically important. Thus, presumably if a conflict materializes between two states, it is not their levels of relative but their levels of absolute capabilities that would, other things being equal, decide the military outcome.

In battlefield terms, many Third World countries can only be said to exist in a condition of substantial insecurity.[21] To some extent, given the substantial variation in size across countries, it would be highly unlikely, though not impossible, that states would balance exactly their absolute capabilities. Our findings show, however, that seemingly no attempts are made to rectify or try to reduce absolute inequalities. Many Third World states, certainly relying on their own resources, could not in fact make an effective military response to one or more of their neighbours and in this respect could be said to be in a condition of insecurity.

A relevant question to which we must turn then is why do states seemingly ignore battlefield security calculations? Though we could not pretend to have the answer, we may offer some possibilities.

In the first place it should be remembered that to eradicate absolute inequalities would be extremely difficult given the enormous variation in size of countries. Some of the larger states would find themselves making very small commitments to the military. Equally, however, it may be recalled that it is not simply that equalization does not take place, but that scarcely any moves are made towards equalization.

Second, larger states have the potential to counter any moves toward equalization. The gap between larger and smaller states quickly becomes such that it can be impossible for the smaller state to match the absolute capabilities of the larger one. The critical point is that the larger state, assuming a sufficient gap, can always undermine any move to equalization by a smaller state by making a matching increase in its military commitment. Thus, equalization presupposes co-operation from the larger state of the form that would require that it forego some development of its military capabilities. Larger states may be unwilling to do this on the grounds that they are quite content with the status quo, in which the smaller states' insecurity is their security. In other words, larger states enjoy, other things being equal, what we might call 'a natural security advantage', which they are evidently unwilling to relinquish.[22]

Third, it is possible that Third World states engage in balance of power strategies which have been the traditional response to absolute inequalities in military capabilities. Certainly there are a number of formal alliances, though these are the exception rather than the rule.[23] It is, however, the case that balance-of-power strategies can be pursued without formal alliances. But there are a series of well-rehearsed problems associated with balance of power strategies, which even if balance of power strategies were followed could render such strategies rather risky.[24] We simply do not know how extensively this mechanism is used, though it is the case that if it is indeed followed successfully then it would reduce battlefield insecurity.[25]

Thus far we have been considering the implication of states apparently choosing to ignore a response in terms of attempting to equalize absolute capabilities. Our second implication continues this line of thinking but focuses rather on the adoption of a response made in terms of equalizing relative capabilities. More precisely we are looking for an argument that might explain why it would be rational for states to focus on security calculations effected in terms of relative capabilities. In other words, if we can make such an argument, then a further reason why states seemingly ignore battlefield insecurity is because they regard it as being less important than another form of insecurity, which may be alleviated by equalizing relative capabilities.

Other things being equal, perceived threat, the basis of insecurity, must be a function not only of level of capability but intent to use those capabilities. We have no measure of intent to use capabilities, nor do we know of any agreed measure to which others may turn in order to measure intent. It does, however, seem eminently reasonable and indeed likely that relative military expenditure is used as a surrogate measure of intent. Though the impact of military expenditure on economic growth is far from clear to academic analysts, let alone to Third World politicians, military expenditure does unquestionably contain readily visible opportunity cost. As any state increases its relative military spending, it is foregoing other expenditure opportunities. It is this idea which lies behind the notion of the military burden, a widely used synonym for relative military expenditure. States may, it seems to us, reasonably interpret military burden as intent, in the sense that a level of relative military expenditure lower than their neighbours would indicate vulnerability on their part and aggressiveness on the part of their neighbours. In effect then as states calibrate their levels of relative military expenditure, they would be signalling to each other a willingness to match a military commitment and a willingness to carry the same burden.

Combining these two implications leads us to an intriguing though tantalizing conclusion. What we do know is that states make harmonizing responses within neighbourhoods to each others' levels of relative rather than absolute capabilities. What we rather tantalizing do not know is whether this produces security or whether it is accomplished by design or default. Thus, if states operationalize security in terms of matching commitments, then the great majority of Third World states achieve neighbourhood security. If, on the other hand, states operationalize security rather more objectively, for want of a better term, in terms of battlefield capabilities, then security is very unevenly distributed across Third World countries. Furthermore, if states do pursue the more subjective form of security, in matching commitments or burdens, then they are largely successful in their designs. On the other hand, this outcome may appear not because it is actively pursued but because attempts to produce battlefield security fail as more dominant states are unwilling to make any lesser commitment than their smaller neighbours. This is what we mean by relative harmonization appearing by default rather than design.

Our third implication, which has an importance in its own right, might also be used to try to unravel the tantalizing issue of whether security is or is not achieved and, if it is, whether it is achieved by design or default. The third implication concerns the question of power hierarchies and relations between capabilities.

In Chapter 3 we discovered some misfit between basic economic capabilities, such as GDP, and military capabilities. Despite strong simple correlations between GDP and absolute military expenditure, we also found that relative military expenditure was not constant across GDP levels. Consequently any hierarchy constructed in terms of GDP would not be replicated in terms of military capabilities. One possible explanation for this result might be that states differ in the utilities they attach to military capabilities. There is in fact a substantial academic literature, to which we return in greater detail in the Conclusion, on the disutilities of military force. Using the ideas of this literature, we might then argue that the failure of relative military expenditure to appear as a constant was a reflection of the decisions reached by a number of states that military capabilities were less important or useful than economic capabilities. This would neatly explain why some states very clearly do not develop the level of military capabilities that they could have on the basis of their GDP. Certainly for those analysts of the conviction that military capabilities carry serious disutilities, the apparent mismatch between military and GDP hierarchies would constitute an important ray of hope in that it would indicate that a substantial number of states had deliberately chosen to eschew military capabilities and, as it were, become willing to accept a lower position in the international military hierarchy than they needed to.

Our results from this chapter provide what seems to us a more plausible and easier explanation. There is indeed a misfit on one level between GDP and military hierarchies as long as we consider this relationship in a global setting across all Third World countries. If we consider the same relationship but examine it within neighbourhoods, then the misfit largely disappears. Thus, the substantial degree of harmony of relative military expenditure within neighbourhoods means that states within neighbourhoods are largely replicating the GDP hierarchy with a matching military hierarchy. In other words, if we focus on neighbourhoods rather than the total population of all Third World countries, we do not find a mismatch between military and GDP hierarchies. Rather than suggesting that some states have explicitly internalized the arguments on the disutilities of military force, thereby accepting downward movement in a global military hierarchy, it seems to us that as far as military capabilities are concerned states focus on neighbourhoods and within these neighbourhoods studiously replicate their GDP rankings in military terms. Far from indicating some acceptance of the disutilities of military capabilities and a rejection of thinking and behaving in terms of power hierarchies, our interpretation, contingent on the necessity of examining military expenditure in neighbourhood terms, would point to a widespread acceptance both of the significance of military capabilities and of hierarchical behaviour.

If we combine this interpretation with our previous two implications we arrive at the following position. As far as military security relations are concerned, states seem to us to respond pre-eminently to the other states within their neighbourhoods and not to a global environment. (This incidentally seems yet another nail in the coffin of the dangers of overaggregating North–South models.) In responding to other states in the neighbourhood environment, states appear to replicate in their military capabilities their GDP hierarchy. In other words, military expenditure is used to institutionalize GDP inequalities and as such economic and military power capabilities far from misfitting actually complement each other. In replicating the neighbourhood GDP hierarchy in their levels of absolute military expenditure, states are led within neighbourhoods to harmonize their levels of relative military expenditure, which is the main result we have observed and have been trying to explain.

Curiously, though much of the analysis of this chapter has been devoted to an exploration of the behaviour of relative military expenditure within neighbourhoods on the grounds that not only did we find coherent results but also we could find no support for an absolute expenditure response, we do finally consider that the absolute rather than the relative response is the more crucial. We are of the view that the harmonized relative expenditure pattern, which does unquestionably appear, occurs by default rather than design. It appears by default, in our view, on the grounds that states seem to model their absolute military capabilities so as to replicate and sustain the inequalities in their economic power capabilities. The consequence of the efforts within neighbourhoods to institutionalize and reinforce hierarchical inequalities is, in the military sphere, the seeming harmonization of relative military expenditure. Consequently, we are inclined to the position that the generalized and high level of security that we might infer from such harmonization is something of a chimera. The more accurate security model would seem to us to be that derived from a focus on battlefield inequalities within neighbourhoods, in which context we are consequently inclined to see a very uneven distribution of security and insecurity across Third World countries.[26]

Notes

1. For some discussion of the concept of security, see, for example: B. Brodie, *War and Politics* (London: Cassell, 1973); H. Bull, *The Control of the Arms Race* (London: Weidenfeld and Nicolson, 1962); B. Buzan, *People States and Fear* (Brighton: Wheatsheaf, 1983); H. Macdonald, 'The Place of Strategy and the Idea of Security', *Millennium*, **10**, 3, 1981; F.N. Trager and F.L. Simonie, 'An Introduction to the Study of National Security', in F.N. Trager and P.S. Kronenberg (eds), *National Security and American Society* (Lawrence: Kansas University Press, 1973); A. Wolfers, 'National Security as an Ambiguous Symbol', *Discord and Collaboration* (Baltimore: Johns Hopkins University Press, 1962).

2. For a fuller discussion of the different levels and forms of security, see especially B. Buzan, op.cit.

3. For general discussion of force and power in an international setting, see e.g. H. Bull, *The Anarchical Society* (London: Macmillan, 1977); M. Howard, *Studies in War and Peace* (London: Temple Smith, 1970); R.E. Osgood and R.W. Tucker, *Force, Order and Justice* (Baltimore: Johns Hopkins University Press, 1967); K.N. Waltz, *Man, the State and War* (New York: Columbia University Press, 1959).

4. A full exposition of the security dilemma is often associated with Butterfield and Herz, though its form, if not the name, had been noted much earlier. For good discussions of the security dilemma, see: H. Butterfield, *History and Human Relations* (London: Collins, 1951); J.H. Herz, *Political Realism and Political Idealism* (Chicago: Chicago University Press, 1951); J.H. Herz, *International Politics in the Atomic Age* (New York: Columbia University Press, 1959); R. Jervis, *Perception and Misperception in International Politics* (Princeton: Princeton University Press, 1976); R. Jervis, 'Cooperation Under the Security Dilemma', *World Politics*, **30**, 2, 1978.

5. If what we term a global absolute response was made we would expect states to adjust their absolute levels of military expenditure in a systematic manner to the absolute expenditure of other states. This systematic adjustment could take either a mutual compensatory variant, whereby smaller states committed proportionately more resources to the military than larger states, or a mutual divergence variant, whereby larger states committed proportionately more resources. The tests would require that logged regressions of military expenditure on GDP for all states produced an R^2 value close to 1.00 with b coefficients respectively less than and greater than unity. The results are entirely unsatisfactory partly because the R^2 value is not close enough to 1.00 and more seriously because the b coefficients are too close to unity. Consequently relative military expenditure is neither negatively nor positively related to GDP, the implications respectively of the mutual compensatory and divergence variants. The global relative response would imply that states adjust their relative expenditure levels to a globally diffused norm. This in turn would require from the regression of military

expenditure on GDP on R^2 value close to 1.00 and a b coefficient close to unity. Though this later condition is largely met, the R^2 value is too low to give us what we really want, namely relative military expenditure approximating to a constant.

6. By neighbourhood we broadly mean contiguous countries, though we make small exceptions to pure contiguity on a number of occasions where this would make sense. For example, we regard Indonesia and Malaysia as neighbours. We do not include either the USA or USSR as neighbours though they are contiguous to a number of countries in our population. We do this partly because their figures would be massively different from our Third World states and partly because they have the capacity to threaten equally not just their contiguous Third World neighbours but any Third World state.

7. Results from other test years are broadly similar and do not corroborate our hypothesis.

8. In Table 8.1, the horizontal axis refers to neighbour size which is the number of states in any one neighbourhood. On the vertical axis: N refers to the total of neighbourhoods of any given size; Sigma S is the tau numerator summed above a given neighbourhood size; Sigma Tau N is the tau denominator summed over a given neighbourhood size; Sigma Tau is the tau value summed again over a given neighbour size. If we sum across all neighbourhoods, then the aggregated tau value is 19/720 = 0.03.

9. There are two main difficulties. First tau can only equal zero if the numerator equals zero, which in turn can only happen when the denominator is an even number. This happens for neighbourhood sizes of 4, 5, 8 and 9. Second, tau can only take a limited number of values when the number of cases is small. For group size of two tau can only be + 1.00; for group size three, tau can only be ± 0.33 and 1.00; for group size four, tau can only be 0, ± 0.33, 0.67, 1.00. Consequently in Table 8.2 we separate neighbourhoods of two and three and argue for no association if positive and negative values balance (it is balance rather than tau values which is critical). In Table 8.3 we consider neighbourhoods of size four or larger. A confounded result, i.e. strong counterbalancing positive and negative results, would occur if the frequencies of both positive and negative results bunched at higher tau values. A true absence of association would occur if tau values bunched either positively or negatively at lower values. This is indeed the result we find. Thus only 22 per cent of cases have tau values greater than plus or minus 0.40. The results for the other test years are similar.

10. A positive residual indicates that a country is spending more on its military than we would expect given its level of GDP; equally a negative residual indicates a lower than expected level of military expenditure.

11. A dyad of course consists of any two states. Thus any one state will be a member of as many dyads as it has neighbours. This raises a potential problem, which stems from the fact that above and below states are calculated across all countries. However, the number of times any state appears in a dyad is of course variable, depending on the number of neighbours it has. If above and below status were systematically related to number of neighbours, let us say states with more neighbours were more inclined to be above, then the occurrence of above would be overstated. This could distort our results. We have checked for this problem both by looking at the distribution of above and below status by neighbourhood size and also by comparing the proportions of above and below status occuring in dyads against the proportions of above and below states. A check shows that the distributions are not skewed and the percentage

occurrence of above and below by dyads and by states are almost identical (in 1982, for example, p(A) and p(B) by dyad and by state are 0.56 and 0.54, and 0.44 and 0.46 respectively).

12. In Table 8.4, the actual distributions are simply the frequencies of the emprical, or actual, occurrences of dyadic combinations. The expected distributions are given by p(AA), p(AB) + p(BA), and p(BB), where p(AA), for example, is the square of the proportion of above occurrences. P(A) and p(B) ideally would each be 0.50. Their values are always close to this, as our logged regressions from which above and below are derived are normal, though they do not equal these values exactly. If there were to be independence in dyadic relations, then the actual and expected distributions would conform. Departures from independence can be assessed by mismatches between the two distributions. In particular we are looking for a propensity for above and belows to cluster separately. This would be shown, as we indeed see, by losses in actual terms from expected occurrences in the above-below dyad. The mean percentage loss over all test years from the above-below dyad is 26 per cent.

13. We have dealt thus far with simple positive or negative residuals to identify above and below status. We can, however, extract rather more information from our residuals. What is especially useful is that since our regressions are logged, then the antilog of the residuals gives the proportionate amount of under- or overspending or the number of times a state under- or overspends.

14. It is important to emphasize the difference between mean values calculated within neighbourhoods across different levels of overspending and mean values calculated separately for under- and overspenders within neighbourhoods across the same levels of overspending. In the former case, we would expect mean values to increase simply because the percentage of cases in neighbourhoods that overspent would increase. In the latter case, there would *a priori* be no reason to suppose that mean values of the overspending and mean values of the underspending states within neighbourhoods changed across percentage overspending levels, unless it were to be the case, which is what we are looking for, that the extent to which states over- and underspend are systematically related as the percentage of cases that overspend in neighbourhoods increases or decreases.

15. The amount of over- or underspending, which we derive from residuals, can be expressed in a variety of related ways. The figures in Table 8.7 should be interpreted as follows. For the overspending states, the figures show the number of times that these states on average spend more than they should. For the underspending states, the figures show the number of times that they should increase their spending to get to the level at which they ought to expend.

16. We give a further illustration to try to ensure the point of the systematic relationship is clear. If we took a neighbourhood evenly divided between over- and underspenders, then we would find that the magnitude of overspending is much lower, on average, than the level of overspending by those states in neighbourhoods where all countries overspend and equally the magnitude of underspending is not as great as that of these state in neighbourhoods where all countries underspend. Furthermore, as we move up the scale, allowing proportion of overspenders to increase beyond the 50–50 split, then the overspending countries will, on average, increase the amount by which they overspend, while the underspending countries will progressively approximate to the point of overspending.

17. The only exception to the argument seems to us to be if military forces could be constructed such that they could only conceivably be used for defensive purposes. If

military capabilities could not conceivably be used against others, then the security dilemma would disappear. This position is actively pursued by some peace researchers though to the best of our knowledge it is not a widely held posture, nor are the practical manifestations of purely defensive capabilities, and they would they have to be totally pure, readily obvious.

18. Jervis, *Perception and Misperception*, op cit., clearly distinguishes spiral and deterrence models and argues, quite convincingly in our view, that neither model is complete in the sense of entirely precluding the other. Security appears to us to contain both deterrent and spiral effects, with each being eminently easily incorporated into security dilemmas reasoning. For illustrations of relevant discussions, see e.g. K. Boulding, 'National Images and International Systems', *Journal of Conflict Resolution*, 3, 1959; J. Burton *Controlled Communication* (New York: Free Press, 1970); A. George and R. Smoke, *Deterrence in American Foreign Policy* (New York: Columbia University Press, 1974); L. Richardson, *Statistics of Deadly Quarrels*, (Chicago: Quadrangle, 1960); L. Richardson, *Arms and Insecurity* (Chicago: Quadrangle, 1960); T. Schelling, *Arms and Influence* (New Haven: Yale University Press, 1966).

19. We have made something of a time-consuming analysis of changes in the composition of neighbourhoods over our test years. We are, however, not entirely satisfied with this analysis and regard it as only preliminary. Nonetheless, we consider it sufficiently developed to support the type of point we are making in the context of the prisoner dilemma. Basically our strategy, in brief, is to classify neighbourhoods in four categories: the co-operative symmetrical (a state is below as are a majority of its neighbours), the competitive symmetrical (a state is above as are a majority of its neighbours), the co-operative asymmetrical (a state is below but a majority of its neighbours are above) and the competitive asymmetrical (a state is above but a majority of its neighbours are below). We examine change from one test year to another. Table 8.8 summarizes these movements from 1966 to 1970 to 1974 to 1978 to 1982.

Table 8.8: Frequency of neighbourhood movements, selected years 1966–82

To	From			
	Co-operative symmetrical	Co-operative asymmetrical	Competitive asymmetrical	Competitive symmetrical
Co-operative symmetrical	80	13	6	7
Co-operative asymmetrical	10	43	1	8
Competitive asymmetrical	6	1	20	7
Competitive symmetrical	9	11	7	72
(N)	(105)	(68)	(34)	(94)

From this table and individual tables covering sets of two test years, we draw the following conclusions. First, any one category shows a greater propensity to stick rather than change. Second, the symmetrical are less volatile than the asymmetrical ones. Third, the propensity for any state to move to a competitive position increases as the proportion of its neighbours that are competitive increases. Finally, the propensity for countervailing movement (i.e. for a country to move in the opposite direction of a move by its neighbourhood) is virtually non-existent.

20. For general discussions of the prisoner's dilemma, see e.g. D. Luce and H. Raiffa, *Games and Decisions* (New York: Wiley, 1957); A. Rapoport and A.M. Chammah, *Prisoner's Dilemma: A Study of Conflict and Cooperation* (Ann Arbour: University of Michigan Press, 1965); T.C. Shelling, *The Strategy of Conflict*, op. cit.

21. In 1978, for example, though similar figures hold for other test years, 45 per cent of states command less than 10 per cent of their combined neighbours' capabilities and 59 command less than 20 per cent. Only 9 per cent of states equal or surpass the capabilities of their combined neighbours. It could be argued that it is unlikely that all of a state's neighbours would gang up against it, the worst case scenario, but even so some 43 per cent of states command less than one-fifth of the capabilities of a single neighbour.

22. The important point or moral here is well captured by the first variant of our general working hypothesis. The variation in size across states is such that, generally speaking, larger states could afford to make a lower relative commitment than their smaller neighbours and still retain an absolute advantage. As we have seen this does not, however, happen.

23. States might also rely on regional collective security agreements. Though obstensibly some such agreements do exist, they appear to be paper rather than practical exercises.

24. For discussions and criticisms of the balance of power, see e.g. H. Bull, op.cit; M. Hass, 'International Subsystems: Stability and Polarity', *American Political Science Review*, **64**,1, 1970; S. Hoffman, *Primary or World Order* (New York: McGraw Hill, 1978); M. Kaplan, *System and Process in International Politics* (New York: Wiley, 1964); K.J. Holsti, *International Politics: A Framework for Analysis* (New Jersey: Prentice Hall, 1967); H. Morgenthau, *Politics Among Nations* (New York: Knopf, 1978); K. Waltz, *Theory of International Politics* (Reading, Mass: Addison-Wesley, 1979).

25. As a corollary to this point we may note that smaller states show no propensity to hold smaller relative military commitments than any of their larger neighbours. If the balance-of-power logic were being faithfully followed by smaller states, it would seem to us that they would be inclined to accept smaller military commitments and, indeed at the extreme, to abandon the military altogether. This unequivocally does not happen.

26. One of the several nightmares in dealing with security, or rather more prosaically one of the factors underpinning the complexity of conceptualizing security, concerns what might be called for want of better terms the subjective and objective dimensions of security. Thus A may feel insecure not because there is any 'real', or objective, threat but because A perceives there to be. If A is convinced of the threat, then the actual or real absence of the threat does not render the insecurity any less real. Equally, a very real threat may exist but not be so perceived by A, in which event there is objective insecurity but subjective security. While it seems to us in principle relatively easy to differentiate the objective and subjective dimensions, the two are horribly interlinked, making it well-nigh impossible to measure separately the objective and subjective dimensions. In our final conclusion to this chapter, in favouring an explication of uneven security, contingent on battlefield inequalities, as opposed to a more generalized

and higher level of security, based on harmonized relative military expenditure, we are coming down in favour of the objective rather than subjective dimension of security. We have favoured this explanation because it fits well with findings in other areas, such as power and hierarchies. However, we would like to be the first to admit we may be quite wrong.

9 Conclusion

This final chapter is written in two sections, the first of which is titled 'Findings and Interpretations'. We have attempted to present our analysis in a coherent and standardized form. Consequently, the most detailed and appropriate summary of our findings is contained in the Summary sections in Chapters 3 and 8. We do not intend to reiterate these sections now. Rather our objective is to provide an overview of a rather more integrated form than was possible as the analysis unfolded in the guise of what we take to be a theory of military expenditure. The second section, entitled 'Evaluation', presents what we may call, for want of a better phrase, a critical appraisal of the implications of the major assumptions underpinning this theory.

Findings and interpretation

We take the principal goal of theory formation in the social sciences to be the production of an interrelated set of tested hypotheses that provide an explanation for a particular area of social behaviour.

A theory may be evaluated, we suggest, in two main ways. First, we may require that it be capable of providing satisfying answers to important questions that may be posed about the patterns of behaviour that describe the area of behaviour. In our particular area of concern, that of Third World military expenditure, our descriptive profile of Chapter 1 has indicated that a military commitment is ubiquitous, enduring but also very variable across Third World countries. The principle questions to which we require satisfying and interrelated answers or explanations are consequently: why is a commitment to the military ubiquitous; why is it enduring; and why is it variable?

The second means of evaluating a theory is to require that it be capable of providing a better set of explanations than any other rival theory. More particularly, this means that it should be able to corroborate more hypotheses than any other theory and/or that we can find hypotheses consistent with predictions from other theories which cannot be corroborated.

A theory consists of three interrelated parts: test results, hypotheses and assumptions. Assumptions we take to be high-level generalized statements whose purpose is to provide a rationale, an integrated and general level of explanation, for the hypotheses.[1] The hypotheses are postulated relationships, which are logically derived inferences from the assumptions. Finally, there are test results, which, assuming they are positive, constitute the corroboration of the hypotheses and thereby of the assumptions.

Though we take theory formation to be a thoroughly praiseworthy objective, we readily accept that theory building is fraught with a number of dangers. It rests very specifically on a particular epistemology, which is not only far from being universally accepted in the social sciences but which also is ultimately defensible only in terms of its own set of values.[2] Furthermore, theory building can come unstuck at any of its three constituent stages. Since each of these stages is inter-related, then problems in any one have ramifications for the others.[3]

We have made this introduction on theory formation not only to try to clarify our objective but also to emphasize that we do not see ourselves as being engaged in the establishment of unequivocal truths. Social science inquiry, as we construe it, engages itself very much more with the production and examination of doubts than of truths.[4]

Five assumptions, outlined in cumulative order, underpin our interpretation of Third World military expenditure.

Assumption 1   Force can be justified, and thereby explained, in terms of two major utilities

Force appears to be not only ubiquitous, in that it is manifested across a host of very different social relationships, but also enduring, in that it is displayed across these relationships over time. Though the substantive manifestations of force vary substantially across different social relations and time and though such social or temporal considerations may influence important elements of force, such as its form or frequency of use, any general explanation of force must be couched, precisely because of its ubiquity and enduring nature, in terms that are independent of social circumstance and time. Conceptualizing force in terms of some basic utilities seems to offer an avenue for providing an appropriately generalizable explanation.

We take force to be simply a subset of the more general set of coercion, whose general appeal is that it permits in principle any party to pursue its objectives. Force is differentiated from other forms of coercion by virtue of its form, namely its use or threatened use of physical means of coercion. Since force is most assuredly not the only way of pursuing objectives, we are presented with the question of what makes force attractive, and thereby justifiable and explainable, as compared with other means of coercion.

The answer is provided by two main utilities, which are distinctive to force. First, force, under certain circumstances, can provide the most efficient means of achieving an objective. If any party has, or thinks it has, a positive balance of physical coercion capabilities over other parties, then force can enable it to pursue its designs *vis-à-vis* these other parties in a faster or more decisive, in other words efficient, manner than other means of coercion. Second, in contrast to this more aggressive utility, force can also offer the capacity to make a response when other responses, based on appeals for example to reason or justice, may be seen to be likely to fail or to have failed.

Assumption 2   The basic building block of the international system is the state

All social systems can be said to contain a political system which at a general level pursue a similar set of goals, structured around survival in an external environment and the resolution of 'who gets what when and how' in their internal environment. The states is principally distinguished from other social systems by virtue of its possession of sovereignty. All non state social systems, in other words, find their spheres of competence or jurisdiction to be in some ways partial or limited. The state, in contrast, is held to be sovereign in that no body exists above it to delimit its authority.

The development of the state, on a more practical level, has taken the form of territorially defined authority systems in the guise of governmental systems. Governmental systems become the principal agent of the state. As such the most generalized role of government is the development and maintenance of a legitimate authority structure capable of sustaining the domestic and external sovereignty of the state.

The state is the basic building bloc of the international system in the sense that it represents currently the most inclusive macro form of social organization.

Assumption 3   The international system, which is quite simply the set of interstate relations, is hierarchical in structure

On one level, the common general nature of the state, together with a common set of general roles, imposes a marked uniformity in the international system. This uniformity, however, does not imply total identity as states can vary in a number of important respects. Thus, governmental systems can vary for example, in terms of their bases of legitimacy, in their structure, or in the more particularized set of goals they adopt. In other words, states can be differentiated according to a variety of different criteria.

The single most important criterion for differentiating states pertains, however, to power, or more precisely to the different levels of capabilities that states can mobilize. Differentiation in terms of the criterion of power capabilities is the single most important form of differentiation precisely because the level of capabilities that can be mobilized by a state is crucial, given that the state is the most inclusive form of organization. States vary substantially in the capabilities they can mobilize and this variation defines the hierarchical structure of the state system. Somewhat paradoxically, while the emergence of the state has induced through the common general form of the state a marked degree of symmetry, the variation in capabilities across states has resulted in a state system characterized by substantial inequalities or asymmetries.

The hierarchical organization of states has a number of important facets of which we note but several. First, a principal preoccupation of any government must be to maintain or improve the position of its state in the international hierarchy on the grounds that the location of a state within the hierarchy is the principal predictor of its autonomy or latitude of options. Second, although the hierarchical organization is enduring the actual location of states within the hierarchy is not. States may move up and down the hierarchy principally in terms of the capabilities they can mobilize relative to others. There is in this respect dynamism within the more enduring hierarchy. Third, the hierarchy conveys very uneven control, which in turn means that states at upper echelons experience a strong strain towards maintenance of the status quo, as in so doing they perpetuate their more privileged position. Finally, the unequal control capacities induce a strong demonstration effect, which diffuses pre-eminently from stronger to weaker states. In other words, more powerful states influence less strong ones not only directly by virtue of controlling the main parameters of interaction but also indirectly through a demonstration effect.

Assumption 4 The international environment in which states find themselves is one of anarchy

The principal difference between domestic systems and the international one centres on sovereignty. While domestic systems can and do break down, through for example external intervention or the failure of governments to establish legitimacy, domestic systems in principle have the potential for establishing sovereignty. There is no counterpart or analogue of domestic government in the international system in the sense that there is no overaching authority structure. This absence is what constitutes anarchy.

Anarchy, however, is not taken to entail chaos. On the contrary, faced with the condition of no overarching authority structure, states can and have evolved a number of mechanisms to try to ensure that international anarchy does not result in chaos or disorder. The principle management mechanisms designed to effect what is often referred to as a 'society of states' are norms of reciprocity, balance of power, and the practice and acceptance of unequal control contingent on location within the hierarchy. International anarchy, an inevitable fact of life given state sovereignty, is not of necessity but certainly can be a highly ordered and managed system.

A particularly important corollary of international anarchy is that, other things being equal, force must play a more enhanced role than in domestic systems by virtue of the lower level of integration characteristic of the international system.[5]

Assumption 5 The military, as a major constellation of force, is both defined by and reinforces the hierarchical and anarchic state centric system

This assumption in effect relates the military to the preceding four assumptions, postulating that the relationship is reciprocal.

While the means of force are most certainly not unique to the military, perhaps the single clearest hallmark of the military is that it represents the largest and most impressive constellation of force. As such a basic explanation of the military is that it affords two attractive utilities.

Militaries, in the form of a distinctive organization characterized by their development and maintenance of the means of force, certainly predate the state system. However, the emergence of the state has not only enhanced the military but led to a particular type of military organization. Technological developments, contingent on economic growth in turn contingent to some degree on the consolidation of the state, have provided the military with unrivalled means of force. Even more importantly and directly, the emergence of the state has produced a permanent, professional and institutionalized military organization of a totally different structure and character from pre-state military organizations.[6]

As well as reflecting the development of the state, the military also reinforces the state. One of the central defining characteristics of the state is the national military, one of whose principal tasks is the protection of sovereignty. By virtue of being dedicated to the maintenance of the territorial integrity of the state, the military becomes one of the principal agents that reinforces the states.

Since a crucial source of power rests with those capabilities based on force, the military becomes one of the primary instruments for defining the international hierarchy of states. Though the hierarchy would not disappear without military organizations, the military not only constitutes a critical ingredient of the hierarchy but also an avenue for upward or downward mobility in the hierarchy. In this respect, neglect of the military means neglect of hierarchical location.

The condition of international anarchy also contributes to an explanation of the military. Even though international management mechanisms exist to obviate any necessity of collapse into chaos, the international system differs in three crucial respects from domestic systems, or more exactly from domestic systems that enjoy a high level of legitimacy. Firstly, force is not a widely used mechanism, domestically, for the promotion of competing interests. Secondly, citizens may rely to a large extent on domestic agencies, such as the police or courts, for physical protection. Thirdly, domestic systems enjoy a high level of integration and institutionalization of interaction. These features are either totally lacking or decidedly more undeveloped in the international system. As a consequence, the international environment is one of substantial uncertainty or ambiguity, which in turn are sources of insecurity. The military offers an avenue for reducing such insecurity.[7]

While international anarchy may encourage the maintenance of the military as a partial response to insecurity, it is also the case that the military encourages and sustains the very anarchy to which it is in part a response. It does so directly by reinforcing the state system, which is the root cause of the anarchy. It also does so indirectly in that any one state's military can constitute a threat to another state. This threat creation, expounded in the security dilemma, further enhances international uncertainty and ambiguity.

In sum, it is important to recognize that the military does not exist in a kind of independent vacuum. Very much to the contrary, the existence of the military contributes to an international arrangement of which it is also a product.

These assumptions provide ready answers to the first two questions of why the military is seemingly ubiquitous and enduring. The widespread development and maintenance of a military would be an inevitable product of the Third World choosing the nation state as a model of development and opting to integrate itself within the international state system. That the Third World should have taken this route is not terribly surprising. One of the ironies of the nation-state system is that it contains a self-destruct element as far as empires and colonies are concerned. The Third World, furthermore, would have experienced a major demonstration effect. Finally, it would be highly unlikely that the Third World, due in no small part to colonial repression, would have proved to be an area capable of radical new innovation and decidedly more likely that it would engage in imitative behaviour. Essentially, therefore, by virtue of assimilating nation-state thinking, Third World countries wrote out their own, albeit copied, prescriptions for a widespread and enduring commitment to the military.

This rather generalized form of reasoning seems to answer quite well the questions of the ubiquitous and enduring commitment. It does not, however, immediately answer the question of why that commitment should be variable. It is to this issue that much of the effort of this project has been devoted.

In Tables 9.1 and 9.4, contained in an Appendix to this chapter, we present a summary statement of results, which have been discussed in detail in the Summaries to preceding chapters.[8] In aggregate, these tables indicate that we can explain variability rather successfully. We are most successful in the case of absolute military expenditure, principally because size, as measured by GDP, plays such an important role. In effect, having discovered this, relative military expenditure, where size is controlled out, becomes more interesting and again we can produce rather successful, though not so impressive, equations.

The critical issue is that the successful predictors of variability must be related to the assumptions we have used to answer the first two questions. In other words, our successful hypotheses, i.e. these which have been corroborated, ought to be logically consistent with or derivable from the assumptions.[9] This, we suggest, is indeed the case.

To conclude this section, we therefore document this consistency in two ways: first by, arguing that the successful predictors are in fact derivable, and, second, by arguing that other potential predictors, which prove unsuccessful, are not derivable.

Though the assumptions, principally because of their rather general form, do not lend themselves to a detailed explication of variability in military commitment (indeed were they so to do this project would be redundant), they would lead us to expect that a certain limited set of predictors would be successful. They would lead us, we suggest, to expect predictors that were generalized as opposed to idiosyncratic, that had a strong international content, and that were closely related to issues of power and security.

This is precisely what we have found and what is summarized in Tables 9.1 to 9.4. Thus, the neighbourhood effect is eminently interpretable in terms of the security dilemma and of neighbourhood hierarchical influences. Interstate conflict is directly tied to security and power considerations. Though domestic conflict may appear to be not so readily congruent, its influence is not as pronounced as interstate conflict, its influence is felt only when that conflict is intense, and finally domestic conflict is directly related to questions of legitimacy without which sovereignty becomes unsustainable. The arms import influence could be expected and interpreted on several grounds. It taps a self-sustaining general military dynamic, or an imported military–industrial complex effect. Furthermore, arms imports, particularly given their changed composition, offer the lure to any state to develop superior capabilities. Or again, arms imports provide a very direct route for a demonstration effect and imitative behaviour. Finally, we found evidence, in the form of the trade diversification measures, of what we have interpreted as a generalized international sensitivity effect.

It is of course essential to isolate successful predictors. It is equally crucial, to our line of thinking, to find unsuccessful predictors. This is so for two reasons. First, our faith in our theory will increase if we can find unsuccessful, though plausible, predictors that we would expect to be unsuccessful. Second, rival theories may often contain overlapping sets of predictors. Our faith will again increase if we can find unsuccessful predictors that would be predicted to be successful by the rival theories.[10]

In this context we find that a host of indicators of economic performance and wealth are unsuccessful. This, we suggest, would be eminently expected by our assumptions. The military commitment would be seen as far too important, as a kind of basic necessity of life, to be responsive to 'fair-weather' or 'luxury-good' ideas consistent with economic performance. Or again, military expenditure is not responsive to sectional interests of the military and through this we have argued to bureaucratic momentum. Again this would be predicted by our assumptions on the grounds that the military is of significance principally in state rather than sectional terms. Furthermore, military expenditure is not influenced by levels of international economic integration. Our assumptions would regard such integration as of mainly tangential concern, which is precisely what we found. Finally, the diffusion of capitalism seems to be an unsuccessful explanation. There are certainly some overlapping concerns between our assumptions and the diffusion of capitalism. Issues of core–prephery or inequality or demonstration effects or domestic conflict are common to both. Consequently, we would expect some of our successful predictors to be consonant with an explanation couched in terms of capitalist expansion. However, there are several factors which are not readily consonant with a capitalist explanation. Thus, sectional military interests are of no import, there is no evidence of any specifically Western influence, and most importantly a military commitment is entirely unrelated to levels of capitalist development, as measured for example by relative wealth or integration into the world economy.

We have now completed the main task we set for ourselves in that we have moved from identifying a complex of descriptive patterns of military expenditure to providing explanations for these patterns. In this context, the immediately preceding arguments would lead us not to conclude that we have a final or ultimate theory of military expenditure but that we do at least have a relatively robust one, containing both pleasingly generalized explanations and empirical corroboration.

Evaluation

Were we to hold a purely mechanistic or deterministic view of social interactions then our analysis could procede no further. Human beings, however, are not simply cogs in some giant clocklike structure but are social engineers. Patterns of social relationships develop and change because human beings create, mould and adapt these patterns. Behaviour, in other words, is a function in part of goals and perceptions. Until such time as all human beings share exactly the same goals and perceptions there can be no one fixed pattern of behaviour; rather there must be competing sets of possible patterns of behaviour contingent on different sets of goals and perceptions.[11]

The activities, associated with theory building and testing, lead us to only to search for explanations of behaviour and to hold these explanations which appear to conform to empirically observed behaviour. The objective of this last section is not to continue this line of investigation but rather to scrutinize the goals and perceptions that underlie the explanations that make up our theory. In doing so we no longer confront the empirical validity of an explanation of the behaviour of military expenditure but rather the validity of the goals and perceptions on which that behaviour is seemingly empirically based.

Though we would not quibble with the argument that force has utilities, it is also the case that force can have disutilities. Development of the means of force carries with it opportunity costs; though force may be temptingly efficient, efficiency is certainly not the only criterion that may be used to select among the variety of means of influence; force holds no guarantee of success; and force may readily be countered by opposing developments of force. In this respect, it could be argued that it is more appropriate to think in terms of net utilities, such that depending on circumstance the balance of utilities of force may be either positive or negative.

That there is substantial evidence for the salience of a state centric system, the second main assumption, is not, in our view in serious doubt. Governments are clearly very crucial actors and states are relatively easy to identify. Governments or even intergovernmental bodies, most of which incidentally conform almost perfectly to state-centric predictions, are not, however, the only international actors of significance. Furthermore, not only are governments themselves often fragmented, i.e. any one government does not behave in a uniform manner, but even governments as a whole are subject to competing pressures and often cannot easily control or subordinate domestic groups. Or again, the idea of a national interest, crucial to the state-centric model, very quickly becomes almost meaningless except in its use as a rationalization for policy. The state centric model requires, however, that national interest has an import well beyond the level of policy rationalization as the basic guide to policy. It is the case, however, that different groups within a state can experience very different balances of gains and losses from any one foreign policy initiative, in which event the idea of foreign policy being a product of the national interest seems decidedly confused. Finally, sovereignty, the single most important root of the state-centric model, is again far from clear. Though *de jure*, or formal legal, sovereignty, which has admittedly important consequences for such features as treaties or membership of international organizations, is relatively clear, the same cannot be said for *de facto* sovereignty. In fact the whole idea of *de facto* sovereignty, which implies that sovereignty is variable, is entirely at odds with the traditional idea of the indivisibility of sovereignty.[12]

That states can be represented in the form of a hierarchy, the third assumption, is again not without foundation but again can be seen in some respects to be an oversimplification. It is not of necessity unequivocally clear which capabilities ought to be included in the hierarchical calculations or indeed how they should be weighted. Or again, state capabilities would be most clear in the context of an autarchic system. As soon as high levels of interchange develop, which is certainly the case in the areas of trade, investment and money, then the significance of individual sets of capabilities becomes decidedly blurred. Or again, capabilities are ultimately of great importance only if they predict strongly to outcomes of power relations. If substantial constraints on capabilities develop, then superior capabilities, the basis of hierarchical thinking, lose their relevance. Finally, hierarchical thinking is of utmost significance only if variation in capabilities across states is taken to be the most important means of differentiating states. If other criteria are used, then this would not of course negate any hierarchy but it would reduce the significance of the hierarchical organization.

That there is no formal world government is certainly beyond dispute. Furthermore, it is quite legitimate, if one so wishes, to define international anarchy in terms of the absence of formal government. What is, however, decidedly more contentious is the interpretation of anarchy so defined. In the first place, the disjuncture between the presence of domestic government and absence of international government is overdrawn. Thus, many intra-state interactions are highly routinized and institutionalized quite independently of government. Or again, many areas of international interaction, particularly in the economic area, are decidedly more integrated and institutionalized than the domestic interactions inside many states. Secondly, the domestic analogy is false and misleading in that domestic governments face a much greater series of demands than is the case internationally. Finally, the mechanisms inferred as necessary to manage international anarchy are not the only possible mechanisms but also inhibit the development of more satisfactory alternatives. The type of management envisaged by those committed to international anarchy is, in effect, quasi central management by the most powerful states. Certainly the liberal conception of a perfect market, however, envisages a situation in which central management is not only unnecessary but also destructive.[13]

The fifth and final assumption concerned the relationship of the military to each of the preceding key components of force, the state, international hierarchy and anarchy. The general reservation in this context is that the relationships are wrongly drawn.

Taking each component in order, there can be no doubt but that national militaries constitute a major constellation of force. The critical issue is whether they constitute a constellation of force with positive net utilities. The disutilities would appear to be substantial. First, force is an extremely primitive form of conflict resolution. Indeed one of the slow but sure transformations of domestic systems has been the substantial investment in efforts to minimize the role of force precisely because of its primitive nature. Furthermore, the international arena has a distinct advantage in this context in that it is much easier to monitor a smaller number of large units than the millions of individuals that may constitute any one state. Second, the maintenance and development of national militaries carries opportunity costs which are substantial in high-income countries and truly glaring in lower-income ones. Third, the technological developments of the means of force appear not only to be endless under the stimulus of the military–industrial–academic complex but to have reached levels of awesome destruction. Fourth, there can be substantial mismatches between military and political victories. In particular, the difficulties inherent in the management of complex, highly differentiated and highly politically mobilized systems render many of the traditional advantages of military victory and occupation meaningless. While militaries may have been useful in dynastic and mercantilist struggles, these days have receded. Finally, although the military may well not be the sole or even the principal cause of war, it is certainly impossible to conduct wars without them. In this respect, the existence of the military may well, even if not encouraging conflict resolution through force, inhibit the development of alternative means of conflict resolution. Furthermore, again though not causing wars, the continuous enhancement of destructive capabilities maintained by the military, together with the enormous constellations of force inherent in national militaries, encourage the increasing destructiveness of war.

There are certainly close historical associations between the military and the emergence of the modern state, in which respect it would seem that the form that national professional military organizations have taken is no accident. The state was not, however, born fully fledged but rather has evolved and changed over time. The principal critical objection to the reciprocal link of the military to the state is that the military reinforces one of the most traditional and increasingly ill-fitting facets of the state, namely the idea that states exist as independent, autonomous entities enjoying sovereignty. While there are many signs of increasing transnationalism and erosion of the sanctity and salience of the state, the military remains as a major pillar of bygone days, ensuring, as long as it remains, that there must be serious limits to international integration.

That a principal ingredient of an international hierarchical model would be military capabilities is again uncontentious. What is decidedly more contentious, in addition to reservations on hierarchical models, is how important military capabilities would be in constituting any hierarchy. Any increase in the apparent redundancy of military capabilities should reduce any importance. Thus, for example, as more states, or more precisely groups within states, commit themselves to the type of issues that have become dominant domestically, such as the promotion of welfare, of development, of the support of the environment, of the development of non-forceful means of conflict resolution, then the traditional subject matter of high politics will become low politics and finally redundant politics. Or again, changing perceptions of the practice of force can again reduce the salience of military capabilities. Thus, for a complex of reasons in this context, two small and insignificant states have stymied in recent years each of the superpowers, in a manner almost inconceivable in the pre-World War II period.

Finally, regarding the relation of the military to international anarchy, it may be argued, first, that the military is one of the principal factors responsible for the negative perception of anarchy. As long as states maintain militaries then it is perfectly rational for any one state to see another state's military as a threat or insecurity. What is happening here is that militaries far from reducing uncertainty are a major source of it. Second, we are caught in a vicious circle in the sense that uncertainty justifies the military which institutionalizes uncertainty which further justifies the military. In other words, the relation of the military to insecurity is such that in institutionalizing tensions and uncertainties, the military writes out for itself a self-fulfilling prescription.[14]

In conclusion, as to where this leaves us, we can only say that it centres on a choice between competing goals and perceptions. If we follow the goals and perceptions contained in the assumptions in the first section of this chapter, which are broadly realist in content, then we may draw several inferences. First, Third World military expenditure is entirely rational. Second, Third World countries are following an eminently expected line of development. Third, in so doing, they are contributing not only to an enhancement of the international state system but are reinforcing one of the principal means for maintaining order in this system.

On the other hand, if we follow the critique of these goals and assumptions, then Third World countries are engaging in a colossal and, in their particular condition, tragic misallocation of resources; they are helping to perpetuate an international system in which they are condemned to the lower echelons; they are reinforcing one of the principal means that sustains the hierarchy and their lower position in it; and they are helping to perpetuate one of the most self-serving, outmoded and dangerous confidence tricks ever dreamed up by the human mind.

Notes

1. We take assumptions ultimately to be empirical statements. Furthermore, with the exception of formal theorizing, the empirical validity of assumptions is critical. An assessment of the validity of assumptions is, however, complicated by two principal factors. First, assumptions can contain stipulations of beliefs, and, second, the level of generality can often be such that empirical testing cannot produce unequivocal results. At the extreme, assumptions can be so general in their form that the principal means of evaluating them rests not so much on direct

tests but on tests of hypotheses derived from them. Despite these difficulties, however, assumptions are crucial in that they provide higher level explanations of operational hypotheses.

2. Theory building, as we construe it, is broadly speaking based on logical positivism, which we see in turn as a particular epistemology, which in turn we see as a set of rules that defines the production of knowledge and consequently a stipulation of what constitutes acceptable knowledge. It is, however, not the only epistemology. It differs from other epistemologies not in its ultimate goal, the production of knowledge which we see as common to all epistemologies, but in the set of rules which defines the means of producing knowledge. It does most certainly have a defence or rationale but since that rationale is contained, as with all epistemologies, in the basic set of rules then the defence is in effect self-justifying.

3. At the testing stage, analysis may come unstuck, for instance, because we use inappropriate test procedures, or unreliable or invalid measurements. Hypotheses may become awry, for example, because inappropriate relationships, in terms of content or directionality, are stipulated. Assumptions can be problematic in containing, for instance, empirical errors. In addition to these, as it were, independent levels of error, there are also possible dangers as the levels become connected. Thus, the hypotheses may not be logically derived or the variables on which the tests are made may be inappropriate operational measures.

4. This may seem a rather strange statement. We take a hallmark of logical positivism to be an explicit recognition of the relatively of knowledge – in other words what may be acceptable at one time may be equally unacceptable some time later. This is principally because logical positivism advances by trying to falsify relationships. If any relationship cannot be falsified at any time, this does not mean it is therefore true. Rather it is simply a corroborated and non-false statement. Somewhat curiously and paradoxically, precisely because the epistemology of logical positivism is so rigorous and critical, it not so much engages itself with doubts but is truly embedded in them. The whole process of analysis is not only subjected to constant scrutiny but the end product is held at best to be but corroborated and relatively valid knowledge. Ultimate and final truths, so characteristic of the nostrum type of production of many other epistemologies, find no place in logical positivism.

5. We take these assumptions to be generally speaking statements of the principal components of realism. Realism is a complex body of thought which has evolved and changed over time. Consequently, there is no single agreed or authoritative realist charter. For a particularly good and succinct presentation of realism, see the chapter by R Little in R.D. McKinlay and R. Little, *Global Problems and World Order* (London: Pinter, 1986). For a selection of some of the main original writings, see: R. Aron, *Peace and War* (New York: Praeger, 1967); H. Bull,*The Anarchical Society* (London: Macmillan, 1977); E.H. Carr, *The Twenty Years Crisis* (2nd edn, London: Macmillan, 1946); D. Fromkin, *The Independence of Nations* (New York: Praeger, 1981); R. Gilpin, *War and Change in World Politics* (Cambridge: Cambridge University Press, 1981); J.H. Herz, *Political Realism and Political Idealism* (Chicago: Chicago University Press, 1951); J.H. Herz, *International Politics in the Atomic Age* (New York, Columbia University Press, 1959); F.H. Hinsley, *Sovereignty* (London: C.A. Watts and Co., 1966); F. Meinecke, *Machiavellism: The Doctrine of Raison d'Etat* (London: Routledge and Kegan Paul, 1957); H. Morgenthau, *Politics Among Nations* (New York: Knopf, 1973); R. Niebuhr, *Moral Man and Immoral Society* (London: SCM Press, 1963); R.E. Osgood and R.W. Tucker, *Force, Order and Justice* (Baltimore: John Hopkins

University Press, 1967); F.L. Schuman, *International Politics* (New York: McGraw Hill, 1948); G. Schwarzenberger, *Power Politics* (London: Stevens, 1964); R.W. Tucker, *The Inequality of Nations* (New York: Basic Books, 1977); K.N. Waltz, *Theory of International Politics* (Reading Mass: Addison-Wesley, 1979; A. Watson, *Diplomacy: The Dialogue Between States* (London: Eyre Methuen, 1982).

6. For a fuller discussion see e.g. S. Andreski, *Military Organisation and Society* (Berkeley: University of California Press, 1971); A. Buchan, *War in Modern Society* (London: Collins, 1968); J.F.C. Fuller, *Armament and History* (London: Eyre and Spottiswoode, 1946); M. Howard, *War in European History* (Oxford: Oxford University Press, 1976).

7. See most of the references in note 5 above or, for an explicit and succinct summary, see M. Howard, 'Military Power and International Order', *International Affairs*, **40**, 3, 1964.

8. We present results for both absolute and relative military expenditure drawn from two- and five-year files. We use five-year files principally to include a measure of conflict measured over time. These equations constitute the single best summary of our results discussed in more detail in each of the preceding chapters.

9. Though we would expect of course to find different answers to different questions, it would seem critical to us that if we have a related set of questions then the components of variables we use to answer any one question must be related to those we use to answer related questions.

10. Generally speaking, unsuccessful predictors (and let us call these for the purposes of this discussion negative findings) are, in our view, seriously and erroneously neglected by much social-science inquiry. Their neglect stems from a mistaken view that if we wish to prove relationships then only positive findings can constitute that proof. Apart from the fact that we disprove rather than prove, negative findings can be just as interesting and important as positive ones. If we construe a theory as a set of independent and dependent variables, then additional corroboration for that theory may be gained by finding independent variables outside that set, that could plausibly be related to the dependent variable, which yield negative results. A negative result only becomes uninteresting if no plausible connection between the independent and dependent variables could be drawn. Furthermore, it is generally speaking rather easy in the social sciences to think up explanations. The much more difficult task is rejecting explanations or more particularly choosing between rival explanations. In this context it is unusual to find competing theories which are disjoint sets. In other words, some independent variables may be common to several theories, indicating that we should be thinking in terms of intersecting rather than disjoint sets. If some predictors are successful and common to two different theories, then we may only be able to choose between these theories by finding some relationships which are expectedly negative to the one but unexpectedly negative to the other. In other words negative findings can play a truly crucial role in selecting between alternative explanations.

11. A common criticism levelled at behaviouralism is that it cannot cope with attitudes, values and beliefs. Since such factors are inherent in human behaviour, then behaviouralism can be condemned to the role of low-level description. The so-called scientific claims of behaviouralism are held consequently to be extremely pretentious. This argument at the outset, is based, in our view, on a red herring in that behaviouralism has never pretended to be an analogue of say physics. The subject matter is quite different and consequently bodies of findings must be quite different. The goal of behaviouralism is not to produce a physics of the social sciences but rather

to isolate and test competing explanations through controlled investigation. More immediately behaviouralism not only explicitly recognizes the importance and relevance of attitudes, values and beliefs in influencing behaviour but also indicates rather directly how we should proceed. Let us refer, for the sake of convenience to attitudes, values and beliefs as subjective factors and other influences on behaviour as objective ones. Then objective and subjective factors may have independent or interactive effects. If we consider government expenditure, then such expenditure may increase because a government, for what ever subjective reason, wants it to increase; equally it may increase because of an objective factor, say, given a social security system, due to a rise in unemployment. Far from ignoring this, a principal task in behavioural inquiry is to examine the relative importance of these two sets of influences. A more complex issue, and one which concerns us more at this stage, relates to interactive effects. Thus, subjective factors are in part a function of objective factors, recognized in attitude research (incidentally a principal concern of one of the major behavioural sciences, namely psychology) as the cognitive component. Subjective factors can influence also objective ones in that they can dictate the objective factors to which individuals or groups pay attention. Furthermore, even if groups or individuals recognize the same objective factors, subjective considerations can lead them to process the objective factors quite differently. At the limit this means it can be well nigh impossible to distinguish objective and subjective factors. Far from invalidating behavioural inquiry, the complexity inherent especially in interactive effects means that such inquiry should not terminate on the identification of a set of explanations. It should explicitly scrutinize the set of attitudes, values and beliefs on which any explained behaviour is based. It should do this precisely because attitudes, values and beliefs do indeed structure behaviour. Thus, if alternative sets of attitudes exist and if such sets can become more prevalent, then behaviour will change. In other words, the type of behaviour, profiled in a corroborated theory, does not of necessity have to endure. That behaviour can change or even cease if the set of attitudes, values and beliefs, on which it is based, changes. It is this type of exercise in which we are now engaged. We are not about to question our corroborated explanation of the military, a task in which we have engaged ourselves extensively throughout this book, but to question the attitudes, values and beliefs on which that behaviour, which in our view exists empirically, is based.

12. *De facto* sovereignty refers to what we might call the degrees of freedom open to governments. If governments experience substantial external constraints on their behaviour, then their options or degrees of freedom become reduced. If such constraints become substantial, then governments' formal legal sovereignty can lose much of its practical significance. While there may be no higher formal legal body, external constraints can play much the same role. Consequently, sovereignty loses much of its content. At the limit, we would therefore be much better off thinking not in terms of absolute and indivisible sovereignty but in terms of decisional latitude, which is variable across governments and time.

13. The libertarian tradition, encompassing anarchism and the libertarian variants of both liberalism and socialism, does not take anarchy to be a deplorable condition nor does it construe anarchy as absence of government. Libertarians are opposed principally to concentrations, and therefore unequal distributions, of power. More positively they wish to promote minimalist governing structures which are seen as the environment in which co-operation can best flourish. From a libertarian perspective, realists are reacting in the wrong manner to a misconstrued situation. Their

management mechanisms, creating in effect a type of interstate centralism, are con-comitantly destroying the basis on which co-operation may develop and substituting in its place a prescription for the institutionalization of conflict. For a varied selection of writings see: M. Bookchin, *Post-Scarcity Anarchism* (Berkeley: Ramparts Press, 1971); R.A. Falk, 'Anarchism and World Order', in J.R. Pennock and J.W. Chapman (eds), *Ethnics, Economics and the Law* (New York: New York University Press, 1982); M. Friedman, *Capatilism and Freedom* (Chicago: University of Chicago Press, 1962); F.A. Hayek, *Law, Legislation and Liberty*, vol.3 (London: Routledge and Kegan Paul, 1979); L.I. Krimerman and L. Perry (eds), *Patterns of Anarchy* (New York: Anchor, 1966); R. Nozick, *Anarchy, State and Utopia* (Oxford: Blackwell, 1974); M. Taylor, *Community, Anarchy and Liberty* (Cambridge: Cambridge University Press, 1982).

14. For a selection of writings covering a variety of the points made in the preceding pages, see: N. Angell, *The Great Illusion* (London: Heinemann, 1914); W. Brandt, *World Armament and World Hunger* (London: Gollancz, 1986); J. Burton, *Peace Theory* (New York: Knopf, 1962); A. Etzioni, *The Hard Way to Peace* (New York: Collier, 1962); J. Galtung, *The True Worlds* (New York: Free Press, 1980); Independent Commission on Disarmament and Security, *Common Security* (London: Pan, 1982); M. Kaldor, *The Baroque Arsenal* (London: Deutsch, 1982); M. Kaldo and A. Eide (eds), *The World Military Order* (London: Macmillan, 1979); K. Knorr, *Power and Wealth* (London: Macmillan, 1973); S. Melman, *The Peace Race* (London: Gollancz, 1962); A. Myrdal, *The Game of Disarmament* (London: Spokesman, 1978); P. Noel-Baker, *The Arms Race* (London: Calder, 1958); C. E. Osgood, *An Alternative to War or Surrender* (Urbana: University of Illinois Press, 1962); G. Prins (ed), *Defended to Death* (Harmondsworth: Penguin, 1983); A. Rapoport, *Strategy and Conscience* (New York: Harper and Row, 1964); B. Russett, *The Prisoners of Insecurity* (San Francisco: Freeman, 1983).

Appendix of summary regression results

The acronyms in the following tables are

GDP	Gross Domestic Product
E	Gross Exports
M	Gross Imports
IL	Gross International Liquidity Holdings
GDPPC	Per Capita GDP
DIVED	Diversification of Exports by Destination
DIVMS	Diversification of Imports by Source
DDC	Presence of Organized Domestic Conflict (as dummy)
DISCI	Presence of International Conflict at Level of Border Skirmish
DISC2	Presence of International Conflict at Higher Levels
DAMTOT	Presence of Arms Imports (as dummy)
OAMTOT	Level of Arms Imports (on ordinal scale)
LNAMTOT	Level of Arms Imports (on interval scale)
MOEN	Average of Neighbours' Military Expenditure as Percentage of Each Neighbour's Expected Value
MOUN	Average of Neighbours' Military Under- or overspending
PE	Exports as Percentage GDP

PM   Imports as Percentage GDP
PIL   International Liquidity as Percentage Imports
RGGDPPC   Rate of Growth of Per Capita GDP
NYDC   Number of Years of Domestic Conflict
TDCO   Number of Years of Organized Domestic Conflict
TDCSUS   Number of Years of Sustained Domestic Conflict
YISC   Number of Years of Interstate Conflict

Table 9.1: Regression results of absolute military expenditure on selected major determinants, selected years 1954–82 – two-year files

	1954	1958	1962	1966	1970	1974	1978	1982
GDP	0.81 (0.64)	0.88 (0.74)	0.67 (0.56)	0.93 (0.70)	0.94 (0.71)	0.84 (0.65)		0.73 (0.63)
E								
M							0.49 (0.38)	
IL							0.27 (0.27)	
GDPPC								
DIVED	−0.01 (−0.23)	−0.01 (−0.31)	−0.004 (0.11)			−0.006 (−0.08)		
DIVMS								
DDC	0.39 (0.32)		0.12 (0.09)				0.13 (0.08)	
DISC1					0.43 (0.16)			
DISC2				0.41 (0.14)			0.20 (0.08)	0.23 (0.09)
DAMTOT		0.33 (0.18)						
OAMTOT			0.19 (0.31)	0.14 (0.19)				
LNAMTOT					0.20 (0.25)	0.18 (0.24)	0.21 (0.28)	0.21 (0.28)
MOEN					0.009 (0.15)			0.001 (0.20)
LMOEN			0.73 (0.29)			0.60 (0.26)	0.37 (0.15)	
MOUN				0.002 (0.23)				
R^2	0.85	0.93	0.95	0.91	0.92	0.91	0.92	0.92
R^2_A	0.81	0.92	0.94	0.90	0.91	0.91	0.91	0.91

Table 9.2: Regression results of relative military expenditure on selected major determinants, selected years 1954–82 – two-year files

	1954	1958	1962	1966	1970	1974	1978	1982
GDPPC					−0.14 (−0.13)	−0.18 (−0.19)	−0.22 (−0.26)	−0.33 (−0.36)
PE						0.29 (0.22)	0.28 (0.20)	
PM							0.29 (0.20)	0.40 (0.32)
PIL						−0.19 (−0.18)	0.20 (0.20)	
DIVED		−0.01 (−0.62)						
DIVMS						−0.01 (−0.26)		
DDC	0.32 (0.50)				0.10 (0.12)			
DISC1	0.37 (0.43)				0.27 (0.19)			
DISC2	0.82 (0.49)			0.27 (0.18)		0.34 (0.30)	0.31 (0.27)	0.23 (0.19)
DAMTOT		0.29 (0.35)						
OAMTOT			0.15 (0.42)	0.12 (0.36)				
LNAMTOT					0.18 (0.43)	0.11 (0.31)	0.16 (0.44)	0.16 (0.41)
MOEN				0.002 (0.59)				0.002 (0.44)
LMOEN			0.85 (0.61)		0.57 (0.44)	0.38 (0.32)		
MOUN							0.001 (0.33)	
R^2	0.57	0.63	0.62	0.61	0.67	0.71	0.77	0.63
R^2_A	0.48	0.60	0.60	0.59	0.64	0.68	0.74	0.59

Table 9.3: Regression results of absolute military expenditure on selected major determinants, selected years 1958–82 – five-year files

	1958	1962	1966	1970	1974	1978	1982
GDP	0.87 (0.71)	0.78 (0.65)	0.73 (0.58)	0.86 (0.64)	0.87 (0.64)		0.74 (0.64)
E							
IL			0.24 (0.20)			0.24 (0.25)	
M						0.46 (0.36)	
GDPPC							
RGGDPPC							
DIVED	0.009 (−0.22)	0.004 (−0.10)					
DIVMS					−0.008 (−0.10)		
NYDC			0.003 (0.08)			0.04 (0.11)	
TDCO	0.063 (0.15)	0.041 (0.10)					
TDCSUS				0.075 (0.14)			
DISC1				0.39 (0.17)			
DISC2					0.21 (0.10)		
YISC			0.061 (0.13)				0.055 (0.11)
DAMTOT	0.33 (0.19)						
OAMTOT		0.16 (0.27)	0.12 (0.16)				
LNAMTOT				0.21 (0.26)	0.12 (0.16)	0.26 (0.35)	0.19 (0.27)
MOEN				0.001 (0.22)			0.001 (0.21)
LMOEN	0.33 (0.15)					0.30 (0.13)	
MOUN		0.001 (0.24)	0.001 (0.18)		0.001 (0.20)		
R^2	0.96	0.96	0.95	0.94	0.92	0.92	0.92
R^2_A	0.95	0.95	0.94	0.93	0.91	0.92	0.91

Table 9.4: Regression results of relative military expenditure on selected major determinants, selected years 1958–82 – five-year files

	1958	1962	1966	1970	1974	1978	1982
PE							0.38 (0.30)
PM						0.40 (0.28)	
PIL			0.31 (0.31)		−0.21 (−0.21)	0.19 (0.19)	
GDPPC							−0.29 (−0.32)
RGGDPPC						−0.010 (−0.17)	
DIVED	−0.012 (−0.62)						
DIVMS					−0.009 (−0.23)		
NYDC							
TDCO	0.052 (0.26)	0.056 (0.30)	0.049 (0.15)				
TDCSUS				0.064 (0.24)	0.046 (0.16)		
DISC1				0.21 (0.17)			
DISC2					0.17 (0.17)	0.23 (0.25)	
YISC			0.081 (0.37)	0.042 (0.16)			0.05 (0.22)
DAMTOT	0.33 (0.40)						
OAMTOT		0.095 (0.36)	0.081 (0.23)				
LNAMTOT				0.13 (0.32)	0.099 (0.27)	0.11 (0.31)	0.14 (0.37)
MOEN							−0.001 (0.43)
LMOEN		0.84 (0.69)		0.60 (0.45)	0.53 (0.47)		
MOUN			0.001 (0.38)			0.001 (0.36)	
R^2	0.76	0.75	0.77	0.72	0.71	0.74	0.63
R^2_A	0.71	0.73	0.74	0.70	0.68	0.71	0.60

Index